William Sharp

Green Fire

A Romance

William Sharp

Green Fire
A Romance

ISBN/EAN: 9783744674058

Printed in Europe, USA, Canada, Australia, Japan

Cover: Foto ©Thomas Meinert / pixelio.de

More available books at **www.hansebooks.com**

GREEN FIRE

A ROMANCE

BY

FIONA MACLEOD

Westminster

ARCHIBALD CONSTABLE AND CO.

1896

' While still I may, I write for you
The love I lived, the dream I knew.'

'There are those of us who would rather be with Cathal of the Woods, and be drunken with green fire, than gain the paradise of the Holy Molios who banned him, if in that gain were to be heard no more the earth-sweet ancient song of the blood that is in the veins of youth. . . .'

'O green fire of life, pulse of the world ! O Love ! O Youth ! O Dream of Dreams !'

THE ANNIR CHOILLE.

CONTENTS

BOOK FIRST

THE BIRDS OF ANGUS OGUE

Hither and thither
And to and fro
They thrid the Maze
Of Weal and Woe:
O winds that blow
For golden weather,
Blow me the Birds,
All white as snow
On the hillside heather—
Blow me the birds
That Angus know:
Blow me the birds,
Be it Weal or Woe!

CHAPTER I

EUCHARIS

'Then, in the violet forest, all a-bourgeon, Eucharis said to me :
It is Spring.'—Arthur Rimbaud.

After the dim purple bloom of a suspended
Spring, a green rhythm ran from larch to thorn,
from lime to sycamore : spread from meadow to
meadow, from copse to copse, from hedgerow to
hedgerow. The blackthorn had already snowed
upon the nettle-garths. In the obvious nests,
among the bare boughs of ash and beech, the
eggs of the blackbird were blue-green as the
sky that March had bequeathed to April. For
days past, when the breath of the Equinox had
surged out of the west, the missel-thrushes had
bugled from the wind-swayed topmost branches
of the tallest elms. Everywhere the green
rhythm ran.

In every leaf that had uncurled there was a

delicate bloom, that which is upon all things in
the first hours of life. The spires of the grass
were washed in a green, dewy light. Out of the
brown earth a myriad living things thrust tiny
green shafts, arrow-heads, bulbs, spheres, clusters.
Along the pregnant soil keener ears than ours
would have heard the stir of new life, the innumerous whisper of the bursting seed : and, in
the wind itself, shepherding the shadow-chased
sunbeams, the voice of that vernal gladness which
has been man's clarion since Time began.

Day by day the wind-wings lifted a more multi-
tudinous whisper from the woodlands. The deep
hyperborean note, from the invisible ocean of air,
was still audible : within the concourse of bare
boughs which wrought against it, that surging voice
could not but have an echo of its wintry roar.
In the sun-havens, however, along the southerly
copses, in daisied garths of orchard-trees, amid the
flowering currant and guelder and lilac bushes in
quiet places where the hives were all a-murmur,
the wind already sang its lilt of Spring. From
dawn till noon, from an hour before sundown till
the breaking foam along the wild-cherry flushed

fugitively because of the crimson glow out of the
west, there was a ceaseless chittering of birds.
The starlings and the sparrows enjoyed the com-
mune of the homestead; the larks and fieldfares
and green and yellow linnets congregated in the
meadows, where, too, the wild bee already roved.
Among the brown ridgy fallows there was a
constant flutter of black, white-gleaming, and
silver-grey wings, where the stalking rooks, the
jerking peewits, and the wary, uncertain gulls
from the neighbouring sea feasted tirelessly from
the teeming earth. Often, too, the wind-hover,
that harbinger of the season of the young broods,
quivered his curved wings in his arrested flight,
while his lance-like gaze penetrated the whins
beneath which a new-born rabbit crawled, or discerned in the tangle of a grassy tuft the brown
watchful eyes of a nesting quail.

In the remoter woodlands the three foresters
of April could be heard; the woodpecker tapping
on the gnarled boles of the oaks, the wild dove
calling in low crooning monotones to his silent
mate, the cuckoo tolling his infrequent peals
from skiey belfries built of sun and mist.

In the fields, where the thorns were green as rivulets of melted snow and the grass had the bloom of emerald, and the leaves of docken, clover, cinquefoil, sorrel, and a thousand plants and flowers, were wave-green, the ewes lay, idly watching with their luminous amber eyes the frisking and leaping of the close-curled, tuft-tailed, woolly-legged lambs. In corners of the hedgerows, and in hollows in the rolling meadows, the primrose, the celandine, the buttercup, the dandelion, and the daffodil spilled little eddies of the sunflood which overbrimmed them with light. All day long the rapture of the larks filled the blue air with vanishing spirals of music, swift and passionate in the ascent, repetitive and less piercing in the narrowing downward gyres. From every whin the poignant monotonous note of the yellowhammer re-echoed. Each pastoral hedge was alive with robins, chaffinches, and the dusky shadows of the wild mice darting here and there among the greening boughs.

Whenever this green fire is come upon the earth, the swift contagion spreads to the human heart. What the seedlings feel in the brown mould, what the sap feels in the trees, what the blood feels in every creature from the newt in the pool to the nesting bird, so feels the strange remembering ichor that runs its red tides through human hearts and brains. Spring has its subtler magic for us, because of the dim mysteries of unremembering remembrance and of the vague radiances of hope. Something in us sings an ascendant song, and we expect we know not what: something in us sings a decrescent song, and we realise vaguely the stirring of immemorial memories.

There is none who will admit that Spring is fairer elsewhere than in his own land. But there are regions where the season is so hauntingly beautiful that it would seem as though Angus Ogue knew them for his chosen resting-places in his green journey.

Angus Og, Angus MacGreine, Angus the Ever Youthful, the Son of the Sun, a fair god he indeed, golden-haired and wonderful as Apollo Chrusokumos. Some say that he is Love: some, that he is Spring: some, even, that in him Thanatos, the Hellenic Celt that was his far-off

kin, is reincarnate. But why seek riddles in
flowing water? It may well be that Angus
Ogue is Love, and Spring, and Death. The
elemental gods are ever triune: and in the
human heart, in whose lost Eden an ancient tree
of knowledge grows, wherefrom the mind has not
yet gathered more than a few windfalls, it is
surely sooth that Death and Love are oftentimes
one and the same, and that they love to come
to us in the apparel of Spring.

Sure, indeed, Angus Ogue is a name above all
sweet to lovers, for is he not the god—the fair
Youth of the Tuatha-de-Danann, the Ancient
People, with us still, though for ages seen of us
no more—from the meeting of whose lips are
born white birds, which fly abroad and nest in
lovers' hearts till the moment come when, on the
yearning lips of love, their invisible wings shall
become kisses again?

Then, too, there is the old legend that Angus
goes to and fro upon the world, a weaver of
rainbows. He follows the Spring, or is its herald.
Often his rainbows are seen in the heavens : often
in the rapt gaze of love. We have all perceived

them in the eyes of children, and some of us have
discerned them in the hearts of sorrowful women,
and in the dim brains of the old. Ah, for sure,
if Angus Og̃ be the lovely Weaver of Hope, he is
deathless comrade of the Spring, and we may
well pray to him to let his green fire move in our
veins: whether he be but the Eternal Youth of
the World, or be also Love, whose soul is youth;
or even though he be likewise Death himself,
Death to whom Love was wedded long, long ago.

But nowhere was Spring more lovely, nowhere
was the green fire of life so quick with impulsive
ardours, as, one year of the years, in a seaward
region to the north of the ancient forest of
Broceliande, in what of old was Armorica and
now is Brittany.

Here Spring often comes late, but ever lingers
long. Here, too, in the dim green avenues of
the oak-woods of Kerival, the nightingales reach
their uttermost western flight. Never has the
shepherd, tending his scant flock on the upland
pastures of Finistère, nor the fisherman lying
a-dream amid the sandy thickets of Ushant,

heard that quaint music—that primeval and ever young song of the passionate heart which Augustine might well have had in mind when he exclaimed, 'Sero te amavi, Pulchritudo, tam antiqua et tam nova, sero te amavi.' But, each April, in the woods of Kerival the nightingales congregate from afar, and through May their songs make the forest like a sanctuary filled with choristers swinging incense of a delicate music.

It is a wonderful region, that which lies betwixt Ploumaliou on the east and Kerloek in the west: the oldest, remotest part of an ancient, remote land. Here the few hamlets and fewer scattered villages are, even in externals, the same as they were a hundred or three hundred years ago. In essentials, there is no difference since St. Hervé or St. Ronan preached the new faith, or indeed since Ahès the Pale rode through the forest aisles in the moonlight and heard the Nains chanting, or since King Gradlon raced his horse against the foam when his daughter let the sea in upon the fair city of Ys. The good curés preach the religion of Christ and of Mary to the peasants; but in the minds of most of these there lingers much of the bygone faith that reared the menhirs. Few indeed there are in whose ears is never an echo of the old haunted world, when every wood and stream, every barren moor and granite wilderness, every sea-pasture and creek and bay had its particular presence, its spirit of good or ill, its menace, its perilous enchantment. The eyes of the peasants by these shores, these moors, these windy hill-slopes to the south, are not fixed only on the meal-chest and the fallow- field, or, on fête-days, upon the crucifix in the little church; but often dwell upon a past time, more sacred now than ever in this bitter relinquishing age. On the lips of many may be heard lines from that sad folk-song, *Ann Amzer Dremenet* (In the long ago):—

Eur c'havel kaer karn olifant,
War-n-han tachou aour hag arc'hant.

Daelou a ver, daelou c'houero:
Neb a zo enn han zo maro !

Zo maro, zo maro pell-zo,
Hag hi luskel, o kana 'to,

Hag hi luskel, luskel ato,
Kollet ar skiand-vad gant-ho

Ar skiand-vad ho deuz kollet;
Kollet ho deuz joaiou ar bed.

But when they had made the cradle
    Of ivory and of gold,
Their hearts were heavy still
    With the sorrow of old.

And ever as they rocked, the tears
    Ran down, sad tears :
Who is it lieth dead therein,
    Dead all these weary years?

And still they rock that cradle there
    Of ivory and gold ;
For in their brains the shadow is
    The Shadow of Old.

They weep, and know not what they weep ;
    They wait a vain rebirth :
Vanity of vanities, alas,
    For there is but one birth
    On the wide green Earth.

Old sayings they have, too: who knows how old? The charcoal-burner in the woods above Kerloek will still shudder at the thought of death on the bleak open moor, because of the carrion-crow that awaits his sightless eyes, the fox that will tear his heart out, and the toad that will swallow his soul. Long, long ago

Gwenc'hlan the Bard sang thus of his foe and the foes of his people, when every battle-field was a pasture for the birds and beasts of prey, and when the Spirit of Evil lurked near every corpse in the guise of a toad. And still the shrimper in the sands beyond Ploumaliou will cry out against the predatory sea-fowl, *A gas ar Gall— a gas ar Gall!* (Chase the Franks!) and not know that, ages ago, this cry went up from the greatest of Breton kings, when Nomenoë drove the Frankish invaders beyond the Oust and the Vilaine, and lighted their flight by the flames of Nantes and Rennes.

Near the northern frontier of the remotest part of this ancient region, the Manor of Kerival was the lighthouse of its forest vicinage. It was and is surrounded by woods, for the most part of oak and chestnut and beech. Therein are trees of an age so great that they may have sheltered the flight of Jud Mael when Ahès chased him on her white stallion from glade to glade, and one so venerably old that its roots may have been soaked in the blood of their child Judik, whom she forced her betrayer to

slay with the sword before she thrust a dagger
into his heart. Northward of the manor, however, the forest is wholly of melancholy spruce,
of larch, and pine. The pines extend in a
desolate disarray to the interminable dunes, beyond which the Breton Sea lifts its grey wave
against a grey horizon. On that shore there
are few rocks, though here and there fang-like
reefs rise, ready to tear and devour any boat
hurled upon them at full tide in days of storm.
At Kerival Haven, too, there is a wilderness of
granite rock, a mass of pinnacles, buttresses, and
inchoate confusion, ending in long smooth ledges
of black basalt, these for ever washed by the
green flow of the tides.

None of the peasants knew the age of the
House of Kerival, or how long the Kerival family
had been there. Old Yann Hénan, the blind
brother of the white-haired curé, Père Alain,
who was the oldest man in all the countryside,
was wont to say that Kerival woods had been
green before ever there was a house on the
banks of the Seine, and that a Kerival had
been lord of the land before ever there was a

king of France. All believed this, except Père Alain, and even he dissented only when Yann spoke of the seigneur's ancestor as the Marquis of Kerival: for, as he explained, there were no marquises in those far-off days. But this went for nothing: for, unfortunately, Père Alain had once in his youth preached against the popular belief in Korrigans and Nains, and had said that these supernatural beings did not exist, or at any rate were never seen of man. How, then, could much credence be placed on the testimony of a man who could be so prejudiced? Yann had but to sing a familiar snatch from the old ballad ` of *Aotru Nann Hag ar Gorrigan*—the fragment beginning—

> *Ken a gavas eur waz vihan*
> *E-kichen ti eur Gorrigan,*

and ending—

> *Met gwell eo d'in mervel breman*
> *'Get dimizi d' eur Gorrigan!*

> The Lord Nann came to the Kelpie's Pool
> And stooped to drink the water cool:

> But he saw the kelpie sitting by,
> Combing her long locks listlessly.

'O knight,' she sang, 'thou dost not fear
To draw these perilous waters near !

Wed thou me now, or on a stone
For seven years perish all alone,
Or three days hence moan your death-moan !'

'I will not wed you, nor alone
Perish with torment on a stone,
Nor three days hence draw my death-moan—

For I shall die, O Kelpie fair,
When God lets down the golden stair,
And so my soul thou shalt not share—

But, if my fate is to lie dead,
Here, with thy cold breast for my bed,
Death can be mine, I will not wed !'

When Yann sang this, or told for the hundredth
time the familiar story of how Paskou-Hir, the
tailor, was treated by the Nains when he sought
to rifle the hidden treasure in the grotto, every
one knew that he spoke what was authentic, what
was true.   As for Père Alain, well, priests are told
to say many things by the good, wise, Holy Father,
who rules the world so well but has never been
in Brittany, and so cannot know all that happens
there, and has happened from time immemorial.
Then, again, was there not the evidence of the

alien, the strange quiet man called Yann the
Dumb, because of his silence at most times—him
that was the servitor-in-chief to the Lady Lois,
the beautiful paralysed wife of the Marquis of
Kerival, and that came from the far north, where
the kindred of the Armorican race dwell among
the misty isles and rainy hills of Scotland? Indeed Yann had been heard to say that he would
sooner disbelieve in the Pope himself than in the
kelpie; for in his own land he had himself heard
her devilish music luring him across a lonely
moor, and he had known a man who had gone
fëy because he had seen the face of a kelpie in a
hill-tarn.

In the time of the greening, even the korrigans
are unseen of walkers in the dusk. They are
busy then, some say, winding the white into the
green bulbs of the water-lilies, or tinting the
wings within the chrysalis of the water-fly, or
weaving the bright skins for the newts: but,
however this may be, the season of the green
flood over the brown earth is not that wherein
man may fear them.

No fear of korrigan or nain, or any other

woodland creature or haunter of pool or stream,
disturbed two who walked in the green-gloom of
a deep avenue in the midst of the forest beyond
the Manor of Kerival.   They were young, and
there was green fire in their hearts: for they
moved slow, hand clasped in hand, and with their
eyes dwelling often on the face of each other.
And whenever Ynys de Kerival looked at her
cousin Alan, she thought him the fairest and
comeliest of the sons of men : and whenever Alan
turned the longing of his eyes upon Ynys, he
wondered if anywhere upon the green earth
moved aught so sweet and winsome, if anywhere
in the green world was another woman so beautiful in body, mind, and spirit, as Ynys—Ynys the
Dark, as the peasants called her, though Ynys of
the dusky hair and the hazel-green eyes would
have been truer of her whom Alan de Kerival
loved.   Of a truth, she was fair to see.   Tall
she was and lithe : in her slim svelt body
there was something of the swift movement
of the hill-deer, something of the agile abandon
of the leopard.   She was of that small clan,
the true daughters of the sun.   Her tanned

face and hands showed that she loved the
open air, though indeed her every movement
proved this. The sun-life was even in that
shadowy hair of hers, which had a sheen of living
light wrought into its fragrant dusk : it was in
her large, deep, translucent eyes, of a soft, dewy
twilight-grey often filled with green light, as of
the forest-aisles or as the heart of a sea-wave as
it billows over sunlit sand : it was in the heart
and in the brain of this daughter of an ancient
race—and the nostalgia of the green world was
hers. For in her veins ran the blood not only
of her Armorican ancestors, but of another Celtic
strain—that of the Gael of the Isles. Through
her mother, Lois Macdonald, of the remote south
isles of the Outer Hebrides, the daughter of a
line as ancient as that of Tristran de Kerival, she
inherited even more than her share of the gloom,
the mystery, the sea-passion, the vivid oneness
with nature which have disclosed to so many of
her fellow-Celts secret sources of peace.

Everywhere in that region the peasant-poets
sang of Ynys the Dark, or of her sister Annaik.
They were the two beautiful women of the world

there. But, walking in the fragrant green-gloom of the beeches, Alan smiled when he thought of Annaik, for all her milk-white skin and her wonderful tawny hair, for all her strange shadowy amber-brown eyes, eyes often like dark hill-crystals aflame with stormy light. She was beautiful, and tall too, and with an even wilder grace than Ynys; yet—there was but one woman in the world, but one Dream, and her name was Ynys.

It was then that he remembered the line of the unfortunate boy-poet of the Paris that has not forgotten him; and, looking at Ynys, who seemed to him the very spirit of the green life all around him, muttered: ' *Then in the violet forest, all a-bourgeon, Eucharis said to me: It is Spring.*'

CHAPTER II

IT was with a sudden beating of the heart that,
midway in Easter, Alan de Kerival received in
Paris two letters : one from the Marquis de Kerival, and the other from his cousin Ynys, whom
he loved.

At all times he was ill at ease in the great
city ; or at all times save when he was alone in
his little study in the Tour de l'Ile, or in the
great circular room where the master-astronomer,
Daniel Darc, wrought unceasingly. On rare
occasions, golden afternoons these, he escaped to
the green places near Paris—to Rambouillet or
St. Germain, or even to Fontainbleau. There,
under the leafless trees of Winter or at the first
purpling of Spring, he was wont to walk for
hours, dreaming his dream. For Alan was a
poet, and to dream was his birthright.

And for dream, what had he? There was Ynys above all; Ynys whom he loved with ever deepening joy and wonder. More and more she had become to him his real life: he lived in her, for her, because of her. More and more, too, he realised that she was his strength, his inspiration. But besides this abiding delight, which made his heart leap whenever he saw a Breton name above a shop or on a volume on the bookstalls, he was ever occupied by that wonderful past of his race which was to him a living reality. It was perhaps because he so keenly perceived the romance of the present, the romance of the general hour, of the individual moment, that he turned so insatiably to the past with its deathless charm, its haunting appeal. The great astronomer whom he loved and served knew the young man well, and was wont to say that his favourite assistant was born a thousand years too late.

One day a Breton neighbour of the Marquis de Kerival questioned Daniel Darc as to who the young man's friends were. 'Nomenoë, Gradlon-Maur, Gwenc'hlan, Taliésin, Merlin, and Oisin,' was the reply. And it was true. Alan's mind was as irresistibly drawn to the Celtic world of the past as the swallow to the sunway. In a word, he was not only a poet, but a Celtic poet; and not only a Celtic poet, but a dreamer of the Celtic dream.

Perhaps this was because of the double strain in his veins. Doubtless, too, it was continuously enhanced by his intimate knowledge of two of the Celtic languages, that of the Breton and that of the Gael. It is language that is the surest stimulus to the remembering nerves. We have a memory within memory, as layers of skin underlie the epidermis. With most of us this anterior remembrance remains dormant throughout life; but to some are given swift ancestral recollections. Alan de Kerival was of these few.

His aunt, the Marquise, true Gael of the Hebrid Isles as she was, loved the language of her people, and spoke it, as she spoke English, even better than French. Of Breton, save a few words and phrases, she knew almost nothing— though Armorican was exclusively used throughout the whole Kerival region, was the common tongue in the manor itself, and was habitually affected even by the Marquis de Kerival—on the few occasions when Tristran the Silent, as the old nobleman was named, cared to speak. But with two members of the household she invariably spoke in Gaelic: with her nephew Alan, the child of her sister, Silis Macdonald; and her old servitor, Ian Macdonald, known among his fellows as Yann the Dumb, mainly because he seldom spoke to them, having no language but his own. Latterly, her daughter Ynys had become as familiar with the one Celtic tongue as the other.

With this double key, Alan unlocked many doors. All the wonderful romance of old Armorica and of ancient Wales was familiar to him, and he was deeply versed in the still more wonderful and magical lore of the Gaelic race. In his brain ran ever that Ossianic tide which has borne so many marvellous argosies through the troubled waters of the modern mind. Old ballads of his native isles, with their haunting Gaelic rhythms and idioms, and their frequent reminiscences of the Norse viking and the Danish summer-sailor, were often in his ears. He had lived with his hero Cuchullin from the days when the boy showed his royal blood at Emain-Macha till that sad hour when his madness came upon him and he died. He had fared forth with many a Lifting of the Sunbeam, and had followed Oisin step by step on that last melancholy journey when Malvina led the blind old man along the lonely shores of Arran. He had watched the *crann-tara* flare from glen to glen, and at the bidding of that fiery cross he had seen the whirling of swords, the dusky flight of arrow-rain, and, from the isles, the leaping forth of the war-birlinns to meet the viking-galleys. How often, too, he had followed Nial of the Nine Hostages, and had seen the Irish Charlemagne ride victor through Saxon London, or across the Norman plains, or with onward sword direct his army against the white walls of the Alps. How often he had been with the great king Nomenoë, when he with his Armoricans chased the Frankish wolves away from Breton soil; or had raced with Gradlon-Maur from the drowning seas which overwhelmed Ys, where the king's daughter had at the same moment put her hands on the Gates

of Love and Death. How often he had heard
Merlin and Taliésin speak of the secret things of
the ancient wisdom ; or Gwenc'hlan chant upon
his wild harp ; or the fugitive song of Vivien in
the green woods of Broceliande, where the en-
chanted seer sleeps his long sleep, and dreams
his dream of eternal youth.

It was all this marvellous life of old which
wrought upon Alan de Kerival's life as by a spell.
Often he recalled the words of a Gaelic *sian* he
had heard Yann croon in his soft, monotonous
voice—words which made a light shoreward eddy
of the present, and were solemn with the deep-sea
sound of the past that is with us even as we speak.

He was himself, too, a poet, and loved to tell
anew, in Breton, to the peasants of Kerival, some
of the wild north-tales, or to relate in Gaelic to
his aunt and to Ynys the beautiful folk-ballads
of Brittany, which Annaik knew by heart, and
chanted with the strange wailing music of the
forest-wind.

In that old manor, moreover, another shadow
put a gloom into his mind. This was another
shadow than that which made the house so silent

and chill, the inviolate isolation of the paralysed but still beautiful Marquise Lois from her invalid husband, limb-useless from his thighs because of a hurt done in the war, into which he had gone brown-haired and strong, and whence he had come broken in hope, shattered in health, and grey with premature age. And this other shadow was the mystery of his birth.

It was in vain he had tried to learn the name of his father. Only three people knew it—the Marquis Tristran, the Marquise Lois, and Yann the Dumb. From none of these could he elicit more than what he had long known. All was to be made clear on his twenty-fifth birthday : till then he had to be content with the knowledge that he was Alan de Kerival by courtesy only : that he was the son of Silis Macdonald, of an ancient family, whose ancestral home was in one of the isles of the Southern Hebrides,— of Silis, the dead sister of Lois de Kerival : and that he was the adopted child of the Marquis and Marquise who bore that old Armoric name.

That there was tragedy inwrought with his story he knew well. From fugitive words, too, he had

gained the idea that his father, in common with
the Marquis Tristran, had been a soldier in the
French army : though as to whether this unknown parent was Scottish or Breton or French,
or as to whether he was alive or dead, there was
no homing clue.

To all his inquiries of the Marquise he received
no answer, or was told simply that he must wait.
The Marquis he rarely saw, and never spoke with.
If ever he encountered the stern, white-haired
man as he was wheeled through the garden ways
or down one of the green alleys, or along the
corridors of the vast, rambling château, they
passed in silence. Sometimes the invalid would
look at him with the fierce, unwavering eyes of a
hawk : but for the most part the icy, steel-blue
eyes ignored the young man altogether.

Yann, too, could not, or would not, confide
anything more than Alan had already learned
from the Marquise. The gaunt old Hebridean
—whose sole recreation, when not sitting pipe in
mouth before the flaming logs, was to wander
along the melancholy dunes by the melancholy
grey sea, and mutter continuously to himself in

his soft island-Gaelic—would talk slowly by the
hour on old legends, and ballad-lore, and on
seanachas of every kind. When, however, Alan
asked him about the sisters Lois and Silis
Macdonald, or how Lois came to marry a Breton,
and as to the man Silis loved, and what the name
was of the isle whereon they lived—or even as to
whether Ian himself had kith or kin living—
Yann would justify his name. He took no
trouble in evasion : he simply became dumb.

Sometimes Alan asked the old man if he
cared to see the Isles again. At that, a look
ever came into Ian Macdonald's eyes which made
his young clansman love him.

'It will never, never, be forgetting my own
place I will be,' he replied once, 'no, never. I
would rather be hearing the sea on the shores
there than all the hymns of heaven, and I would
rather be having the canna and the heather
over my head than be under the altar of the
great church at Kerloek. No, no, it is the pain
I have for my own place, and the isle where my
blood has been for hundreds of years, and where
for sure my heart is, Alan Mac——'

With eager ears Alan had hoped for the name whereat the old man had stopped short. It would have told him much. 'Alan, son of —— !' Even that baptismal name would probably have told him if his father were a Gael or a Breton, an Englishman or a Frenchman. But Yann said no. more, then or later.

Alan had hoped, too, that when he came back after his first long absence from Kerival, his aunt would be more explicit with him. A vain hope ; for when once more he was at the château he found the Marquise even less communicative than was her wont. Her husband was more than ever taciturn, and a gloom seemed to have descended upon the house. For the first time he noticed a change in the attitude of Annaik. Her great, scornful, wild-bird eyes looked at him often strangely. She sought him, and then was silent. If he did not speak, she became morose: if he spoke, she relapsed into her old scornful quiescence. Sometimes, when they were alone, she unbent, and was his beautiful cousin and comrade again: but in the presence of Ynys she bewildered him by her sudden *ennui*, or bitterness, or even shadowy hostility. As for Ynys, she was unhappy, save in Alan's love —a love that neither her father nor mother knew, and of which she never spoke to Annaik.

If Alan were a dreamer, Ynys was even more so. Then, too, she had what Annaik had not, though she lacked what her sister had. For she was mystical as that young saint of the Bretons who saw Christ walking by night upon the hills, and believed that he met there a new Endymion, his Bride of the Church come to him in the moonshine. Ynys believed in St. Guennik, as she believed in Jeanne d'Arc, and no legend fascinated her more than that strange one she had heard from Yann, of how Arthur the Celtic hero would come again out of Flath-innis, and redeem his lost receding peoples. But, unlike Annaik, she had little of the barbaric passion, little of that insatiate nostalgia for the life of the open moor and the windy sea, though these she loved not less whole-heartedly than did her sister. The two both loved nature as few women love her: but to Annaik the forest and the moorland were home, while to Ynys they

were rather sanctuaries or realms of natural
romance.

This change to an unwelcome taciturnity had
been noted by Alan on his home visit at Christ-
mas. Still, he had thought little of it after his
return to Paris, for the Noel-tide had been
sweetened by the word given to him by Ynys.

Then Easter had come, and with it the two
letters of such import. That from the Marquise
was short and in the tongue he and she loved
best: but even thus it was written guardedly.
The purport was that, now his twenty-fifth birthday was at hand, he would soon learn what he
had so long wished to know.

That from Ynys puzzled him. Why should
dispeace have arisen between Ynys and Annaik?
Why should an already gloomy house have been
made still more sombre?

One day, Ynys wrote, she had come upon
Annaik riding Sultan, the black stallion, and
thrashing the horse till the foam flew from the
champed bit. When she had cried to Annaik
to be merciful, and asked her why she punished

Sultan so, her sister had cried mockingly, 'It is my Love! *Addio, Amore! Addio! Addio! Addio!*'—and at each *addio* had brought her whip so fiercely upon the stallion's quivering flanks that he had reared, and all but thrown her, till she swung him round as on a pivot and went at a wild gallop down a long beech alley that led into the heart of the forest.

Well, these things would be better understood soon. In another week he would be out of Paris, possibly never to return. And then . . . Brittany—Kerival—Ynys!

Nevertheless his heart was not wholly away from his work. The great astronomer had known and loved Hersart de Kerival, the younger brother of Tristran, and it was for his sake that he had taken the young man into his observatory. Soon he had discovered that the youth loved the beautiful science, and was apt, eager, and yet patient to learn. In the five years which Alan spent—with brief Brittany intervals —in the Observatory of the Tour de l'Ile, he had come to delight in the profession which he had chosen, and of which the Marquise had approved.

He was none the less close and eager a student
because that he brought to this enthralling science
that spirit of the poetry of the past, which was
the habitual atmosphere wherein his mind dwelt.
Even the most eloquent dissertations of Daniel
Darc failed to move him so much as some ancient
strain wherein the stars of heaven were hailed as
kindred of men : and never had any exposition of
the lunar mystery so exquisitely troubled him as
that wonderful cry of Ossian which opens the
poem of *Darthula* :—

‘ Daughter of heaven, fair art thou ! the silence of thy
face is pleasant. Thou comest forth in loveliness : the
stars attend thy blue steps in the east. The clouds rejoice
in thy presence, O moon, and brighten their dark-brown
sides. Who is like thee in heaven, daughter of the night?
The stars are ashamed in thy presence, and turn aside
their green sparkling eyes. Whither dost thou retire
from thy course, when the darkness of thy countenance
grows? Hast thou thy hall like Ossian ? Dwellest thou
in the shadow of grief? Have thy sisters fallen from
heaven? Are they who rejoiced with thee, at night, no
more ?—Yes !—They have fallen, fair light ! and thou
dost often retire to mourn. But thou thyself shalt fail,
one night ; and leave thy blue path in heaven. The stars
will then lift their green heads : they, who were ashamed
in thy presence, will rejoice.’

CHAPTER III

Yes, he was glad to leave Paris, although that home of lost causes, thus designate in a far truer sense than is the fair city by the Isis, had a spell for him. But not Paris, not even what, night after night, he beheld from the Tour de l'Ile, held him under a spell comparable with that which drew him back to the ancient land where his heart was.

In truth it was with relief at last that he saw the city recede from his gaze, and merge into the green alleys north-westward. With a sigh of content, he admitted it was indeed well to escape from that fevered life—a life that, to him, even in his lightest mood, seemed far more phantasmal than that which formed the background to all his thoughts and visions. Long

before the cherry orchards above Rouen came
into view, he realised how glad he was even to be
away from the bare, gaunt room where so many
of his happiest hours had been spent: that
windy crow's-nest of a room at the top of the
Tour de l'Ile, whence nightly he had watched
the procession of the stars, and nightly had
opened the dreamland of his imagination to an
even more alluring procession out of the past.

His one regret was in having to part from Daniel
Darc, that strange and impressive personality
who had so fascinated him, and the spell of
whose sombre intellect, with its dauntless range
and scope, had startled the thought of Europe,
and even given dreams to many to whom all
dreams had become the very Fata Morgana of
human life.

Absorbed as he was, Daniel Darc realised that
Alan was an astronomer primarily because he was
a poet, rather than an astronomer by inevitable bias. He saw clearly into the young man's
mind, and certainly did not resent that his
favourite pupil loved to dwell with Merlin rather
than with Kepler, and that even Newton or his

own master Arago had no such influence over him
as the far off, nigh inaudible music of the harp of
Aneurin.

And in truth below all Alan's passion for
science, of that science which is at once the
oldest, the noblest, and the most momentous :
the science of the innumerous concourse of dead,
dying, and flaming adolescent worlds—dust about
the threshold of an unfathomable and immeasurable universe, wherein this earth of ours is no
more than a mere whirling grain of sand—below
all this living devotion lay a deeper passion
still.

Truly, his soul must have lived a thousand
years ago. In him, at least, the old Celtic brain was
reborn with a vivid intensity which none guessed
and none except Ynys knew—if even she, for Alan
himself only vaguely surmised the extent and
depth of this obsession. In heart and brain that
old world lived anew. Himself a poet, all that
was fair and tragically beautiful was for ever
undergoing in his mind a marvellous transfor-
mation—a magical resurrection rather, wherein
what was remote and bygone, and crowned with

oblivious dust, became alive again with intense and beautiful life.

It did not harmonise ill with Alan's mood, that, on the afternoon of the day he left Rouen, great bulbous storm-clouds soared out of the west, and cast a gloom upon the landscape.

That is a strange sophistry which registers passion according to its nearness to the blithe weal symbolised in fair weather.   Deep passion instinctively moves towards the shadow rather than towards the golden noons of light.   Passion hears what love at the most dreams of: passion sees what love mayhap dimly discerns in a glass darkly.   A million of our fellows are 'in love' at any or every moment; and for these the shadowy way is intolerable.   But for the few, in whom love is, the eyes are circumspect against the dark hour which comes when heart and brain and blood are aflame with the paramount ecstasy of life.

Deep passion is always in love with death. The temperate solicitudes of affection know not this perverse emotion, which is simply the darker shadow inevitable to a deeper joy—as the profundity of an Alpine lake is to be measured by the height of the remote summits which rise sheer from its marge.

When Alan saw this gloom slowly absorb the sunlight, and heard below the soft Spring cadences of the wind the moan of coming tempest, his melancholy lightened. Soon he would see the storm crushing through the woods of Kerival: soon feel the fierce rain come sweeping inland from Ploumaliou: soon hear, confusedly obscure, the noise of the Breton Sea along the reef-set sands. Already he felt the lips of Ynys pressed against his own.

The sound of the sea called through the dusk, now with the muffled under-roar of famished lions, now with a loud, continuous baying like that of eager hounds.

Seaward, the deepening shadows passed intricately from wave to wave. The bays and sheltered waters were full of a tumult as of baffled flight, of fugitives jostling each other in a wild and fruitless evasion. Along the interminable reach of the dunes of Kerival the sea's lip writhed

and curled; while out of the heart of the turbu-
lent waste beyond issued a shrill, intermittent
crying, followed by stifled laughter. Ever and
again tons of whirling water, meeting, disparted
with a hoarse thunder. This ever growing and
tempestuous violence was reiterated in a myriad
rancous, clamant voices along the sands, and
among the reefs and rocks and weed-covered,
wave-hollowed crags.

Above the shore a ridge of tamarisk-fringed
dune suspended, hanging there, dark and dishevelled, like a gigantic eyebrow on the forehead of a sombre and mysterious being. Beyond
this, again, lay a stretch of barren moor, caught
and clasped a mile away by a dark belt of pines,
amid which the incessant volume of the wind
passed with a shrill whistling. Farther in
among the trees were oases of a solemn silence,
filled only at intervals with a single flute-like
wind-eddy, falling there as the song of a child
lost and baffled in a waste place.

Over and above the noise of the sea was
a hoarse cry thridding it as a flying shuttle in
a gigantic loom. This was the wind, which

continuously swept from wave to wave, shrewd, salt, bitter with the sterile breath of the wilderness whereon it roamed, crying and moaning, baying, howling, insatiate.

The sea-fowl, congregating from afar, had swarmed inland. Their wailing cries filled the spray-wet obscurities. The blackness that comes before the deepest dark lay in the hollow of the great wings of the tempest. Peace nowhere prevailed, for in those abysmal depths where the wind was not even a whisper, there was listless gloom only, because no strife is there, and no dream lives amid those silent apathies.

Neither upon the waters nor on the land was there sign of human life. In that remote region, solitude was not a dream but a reality. An ancient land, this loneliest corner of sea-washed Brittany : an ancient land, with ever upon it the light of olden dreams, the gloom of indefinable tragedy, the mystery of a destiny long ago begun and never fulfilled.

Lost like a rock in a forest, a weather-worn ivy-grown château stood within sound though not within sight of this tempestuous sea. All about it was the deep sonorous echo of wind and wave, transmuted into a myriad cries among the wailing pines and oaks and vast beeches of the woods of Kerival. Wind and wave, too, made themselves audible amid the gables and in the huge chimneys of the old manor-house : even in the draughty corridors an echo of the sea could be heard.

The pathways of the forest were dank with sodden leaves, the debris of Autumn which the snows of Winter had saved from the whirling gales of January. Underneath the brushwood and the lower boughs these lay in brown, clotted masses, emitting a fugitive indefinite odour, as though the ghost of a dead year passed in that damp and lifeless effluence. But along the frontiers of the woods there was an eddying dust of leaves and small twigs, and part at least of the indeterminate rumour which filled the air was caused by this frail lapping as of innumerable minute wings.

In one of those leaf-quiet alleys, shrouded in a black-green darkness save where in one spot the gloom was illumined into a vivid brown, because of a wandering beam of light from a turret in the château, a man stood. The head was forwardly inclined, the whole figure intent as a listening animal. He and his shadow were as those flowers of darkness whose nocturnal bloom may be seen of none save in the shadowy land of dream.

When for a moment the wind-wavered beam of light fell athwart his face—so dark and wild that he might well have been taken for a nameless creature of the woods—he moved.

With a sudden gesture he flung his arms above his head. His shadow sprang to one side with fantastic speed, leaping like a diver into the gulf of darkness.

' Annaik ! ' he cried. ' Annaik, Annaik ! '

The moan of the wind out of the sea, the confused noise of the wind's wings baffling through the woods : no other answer than these, no other sound.

' Annaik, Annaik ! '

There was pain as of a wounded beast in the harsh cry of this haunter of the dark : but the next moment it was as though the lost shadow had leapt back, for a darkness came about the

man, and he lapsed into the obscurity as a wave
sinks into a wave.

But, later, out of the silence came a voice.

'Ah, Annaik!' it cried, 'ah, Annaik, forsooth!
It is Annaik of Kerival you are, and I the dust
upon the land of your fathers—but, by the blood
of Ronan, it is only a woman you are; and, if I
had you here, it is a fall of my fist you would be
having, ay, the stroke and the blow, for all that
I love you as I do, white woman, ay, and curse
you and yours for that loving!'

Then, once again, there was silence. Only the
screeching of the wind among the leaves and
tortured branches, only the deep roar of the
tempest at the heart of the forest, only the
thunder of the sea throbbing pulse-like through
the night. Nor when, a brief while later, a
white owl, swifter but not less silent than a drift
of vapour, swooped that way, was there living
creature in that solitary place.

The red-yellow beam still turned into brown
the black-green of that windy alley; but the
man, and the shadow of him, and the pain of the
beast that was in him, and the cry of the baffled

soul, the cry that none might know or even guess, of all this sorrow of the night nothing remained save the red light lifting and falling through the shadowy hair of what the poets of old called the Dark Woman . . . Night.

Only, who may know if in that warmth and glow within the House of Kerival, some sudden menace from the outside world of life did not knock at the heart of Annaik, where she, tall and beautiful in her cream-white youth, and with her mass of tawny hair, stood by Ynys, whose dusky loveliness was not less than her own—both radiant in the firelight, with laughter upon the lips, and light within their eyes.

O flame that burns where fires of home are lit: and O flame that burns in the heart to whom life has not said, Awake: and O flame that smoulders from death to life, and from life to death, in the dumb lives of those to whom the primrose way is closed ! Everywhere the burning of the burning, the flame of the flame : pain and the shadow of pain, joy, and the rapt breath of joy, flame of the flame that, burning, destroyeth not till the flame is no more.

It was the night of the home-coming of Alan.
So long had Ynys and Annaik looked forward to
this hour, that now hardly could they believe
the witness of their eyes when with eager glances
they scrutinised the new comer—their Alanik
of old.

He stood before the great fire of logs. Upon
his face the sharp, damp breath of the storm still
lingered, but in his eyes was a light brighter
than any dancing flame would cause, and in his
blood a pulse that leaped because of another
reason than that swift ride through the stormy
woods of Kerival.

At the red and stormy break of that day
Ynys had awaked with a song of joy in her
heart, that from hour to hour had found expression in birdlike carollings, little words and
fugitive phrases which rippled from her lips, the
sunshine-spray from the fount of life whereon
her heart swam as a nenuphar on an upwelling
pool. Annaik also had waked at that dawn of
storm. She had risen in silence, and in silence
had remained all day, giving no sign that the
flame within her frayed the nerves of her heart.

Throughout the long hours of tempest, and into that dusk wherein the voice of the sea moved moaning across the land, laughter and dream had alternated with Ynys. Annaik looked at her strangely at times, but said nothing. Once, standing in the twilight of the dark-raftered room, Ynys clasped her hands across her bosom and murmured, ' O heart be still: my heaven is come.' And in that hour, and in that place, she who was twin to her—strange irony of motherhood, that should give birth in one hour to Day and Night, for even as day and night were these twain, so unlike in all things— in that hour and in that place, Annaik also clasped her hands across her bosom, and the words that died across the shadow of her lips were, ' O heart be still: my hell is near.'

And now he for whom both had waited, stood, flooded in the red fireglow which leaped from panel to panel, and from rafter to rafter, while, without, the howling of the wind rose and fell in prolonged monotonous cadences—anathemas rather, whirled through a darkness full of be-wilderment and terror.

As for Alan, it was indeed for joy to him to
stand there, home once more, with not only the
savagery of the tempest behind him, but, also left
behind, that unspeakably far off, bewilderingly remote city of Paris whence he had so swiftly come.

It is said of an ancient poet of the druid days
that he had the power to see the lives of the
living, and these as though they were phantoms,
separate from the body.   Was there not a young
king of Albainn who, in a perilous hour, discovered this secret of old time, and knew how a
life may be hidden away from the body so that
none may know of it, save the wind that whispers
all things, and the tides of day and night which
bear all things upon their dark flood ?

King of Albainn, poet of the old time, not
alone three youthful dreamers would you have
seen there, in that storm-beset room.   For there
you would have seen six figures standing side by
side.   Three of these would have been Alan de
Kerival, and Ynys the Dark, and Annaik the
Fair : and of the other three, one would be of a
dusky-haired woman with starry, luminous eyes ;
and one a pale woman with a wealth of tawny

hair, with eyes aflame, meteors in a desert place;
and one a man young and strong and fair to see
as Alan de Kerival, but round about him a
gloom, and through that gloom his eyes as stars
seen among the melancholy hills.

Happy laughter of the world that is always
young—happy, in that we are not all seers of old
or kings of Albainn! For who, looking into the
mirrors of Life and seeing all that is to be seen,
would look again, save those few to whom Life
and Death have come sisterly and whispered the
secret that some have discerned, how these twain
are one and the same.

Nevertheless, in that happy hour for him,
Alan saw nothing of what Ynys feared. Annaik
had abruptly yielded to a strange gaiety, and
her swift laugh and gypsy smile made his heart
glad.

Never had he seen, even in Paris, women more
beautiful. Deep-set as his heart was in the
beauty of Ynys, he found himself admiring that
of Annaik with new eyes. Truly, she was just
such a woman as he had often imagined when
Ian had recited to him the ballad of the Sons of

Usna or that of how Dermid and Graine fled from
the wrath of Fionn.

And they, too, looking at their tall cousin, with
his wavy brown hair, broad low brows, grey-blue
eyes, and erect carriage, thought him the comeliest man to be seen in France; and each in
her own way was proud and glad, though one,
also, with killing pain.

CHAPTER IV

Soon after supper, Annaik withdrew. Ynys and Alan were glad to be alone, and yet Annaik's absence perturbed them. In going she bade good-night to her cousin, but took no notice of her sister.

At first the lovers were silent, though they had much to say, and in particular Alan was anxious to know what it was that Ynys had alluded to in her letter when she warned him that unforeseen difficulties were about their way.

It was pleasant to sit in that low-roofed dark old room, and feel the world fallen away from them. Hand in hand they looked at each other lovingly, or dreamed into the burning logs, seeing there all manner of beautiful visions. Outside, the wind still moaned and howled, though with less of savage violence, and the rain had ceased.

For a time Ynys would have no talk of Kerival; Alan was to tell all he could concerning his life in Paris, what he had done, what he had dreamed of, and what he hoped for now. But at last he laughingly refused to speak more of himself, and pressed her to reveal what had been a source of anxiety.

'You know, dear,' she said, as she rose and leaned against the mantelpiece, her tall figure and dusky hair catching a warm glow from the fire, 'you know how pitiable is this feud between my father and mother—how for years they have seen next to nothing of each other; how they live in the same house and yet are strangers. You know, too, how more than ever unfortunate this is, for themselves, and for Annaik and me, on account of our mother being an invalid, and of our father being hardly less frail. Well, I have discovered that the chief, if not indeed the only, abiding source of misunderstanding is *you*, dear Alan!'

'But why, Ynys?'

'Ah, why? That is, of course, what I cannot tell you. Have you no suspicion, no idea?'

'None. All I know is that M. de Kerival allows me to bear his name, but that he dislikes, if, indeed, he does not actually hate me.'

'There is some reason. I came upon him talking to my mother a short time ago. She had told him of your imminent return.

' " I never wish to see his face," my father cried with fierce vehemence: then, seeing me, he refrained.'

'Well, I shall know all the day after to-morrow. Meanwhile, Ynys, we have the night to ourselves. Dear, I want to learn one thing. What does Annaik know? Does she know that we love each other? Does she know that we have told each other of this love, and that we are secretly betrothed?'

'She *must* know that I love you, and sometimes I think she knows that you love me. But . . . O Alan, I am so unhappy about it! . . . I fear that Annaik loves you also, and that this will come between us all. It has already frozen her to me and me to her.'

Alan looked at Ynys with startled eyes. He knew Annaik better than any one did; and he dreaded the insurgent bitterness of that wild and wayward nature. Moreover, in a sense he loved her, and it was for sorrow to him that she should suffer in a way wherein he could be of no help.

At that moment the door opened, and Matieu, a white-haired old servant, bowing ceremoniously, remarked that Monsieur le Marquis desired to see Mamzell Ynys immediately.

Ynys glanced round, told Matieu that she would follow, and then turned to Alan. How beautiful she was, he thought: more and more beautiful every time he saw her. Ah, fair mystery of love, which puts a glory about the one loved; a glory that is no phantasmal light, but the realised beauty evoked by seeing eyes and calling heart.

On her face was a wonderful colour, a delicate flush that came and went. Again and again she made a characteristic gesture, putting her right hand to her forehead and then through the shadowy wavy hair which Alan loved so well and ever thought of as the fragrant dusk. How glad he was that she was tall and lithe, graceful as a young birch; that she was strong and kissed brown and sweet of sun and wind; that her beauty was old as the world, and fresh as every dawn, and new as each recurrent Spring. No wonder he was a poet, since Ynys was the living poem who inspired all that was best in his life, all that was fervent in his brain.

Thought, kindred to this, kept him a long while by the fire in deep reverie, after Ynys had thrilled him by her parting kisses, and had gone to her father. He realised, then, how it was she gave him the sense of womanhood as no other woman had done. In her, he recognised the symbol as well as the individual. All women shared in his homage because of her. His deep love for her, his ever-growing passion, could evoke from him a courtesy, a chivalry, towards all women which only the callous or the coarse failed to note. She was his magic. The light of their love was upon everything; everywhere he found synonyms and analogues of 'Ynys.' Deeply as he loved beauty, he had learned to love it far more keenly and understandingly, because of her. He saw now through the accidental, and everywhere discerned the eternal beauty, the echoes of whose wandering are in every heart and brain, though few discern the white vision or hear the haunting voice.

And with his love had come knowledge of many things hidden from him before. Sequences were revealed where he had perceived only blind inconsequence. Nature became for him a scroll, a palimpsest with daily mutations. With each change he found a word, a clue, leading to the fuller elucidation of that primeval knowledge which, fragmentarily, from age to age has been painfully lost, regained and lost again, though never yet wholly irrecoverable.

Through this new knowledge, too, he had come to understand the supreme wonder and promise, the supreme hope of our human life, in the mystery of motherhood. All this and much more he owed to Ynys, and to his love for her. She was all that a woman can be to a man. In her he found the divine abstractions which are the beacons of the human soul in its obscure wayfaring—Romance, Love, Beauty. It was not enough that she gave him romance, that she gave him love, that she was the most beautiful of women in his eyes. When he thought of the one, it was to see the starry eyes and to hear the charmed voice of Romance herself, in the voice and in the eyes of Ynys; when he thought of Love it was to hear Ynys's heart beating, to listen to the secret rhythms in Ynys's brain, to feel the life-giving sunflood that was in her pure but intense and glowing passion.

Thus it was that she had for him that immutable attraction which a few women have for a few men: an appeal, a charm, that atmosphere of romance, that air of ideal beauty, wherein lies the secret of all passionate art. The world without wonder, the world without mystery! That indeed is the rainbow without colours, the sunrise without living gold, the noon void of light.

To him, moreover, there was but one woman. In Ynys he had found her. This exquisite prototype was at once a child of nature, a beautiful pagan, a daughter of the sun, was at once this and a soul alive with the spiritual life, intent upon the deep meanings lurking everywhere, wrought to wonder even by the common habitudes of life, to mystery even by the familiar and the explicable. Indeed, the mysticism which was part of the spiritual inheritance come with her northern strain was one of the deep bonds which united them.

What if both at times were wrought too deeply by this beautiful dream? What if the inner life triumphed now and then, and each forgot the deepest instinct of life, that here the body is overlord and the soul but a divine consort? There are three races of man. There is the myriad race which loses all, through (not bestiality, for the brute world is clean and sane) perverted animalism; and there is the myriad race which denounces humanity, and pins all its faith and joy to a life the very conditions of whose existence are incompatible with the law to which we are subject, the sole law, the law of nature. Then there is that small untoward clan, which knows the divine call of the spirit through the brain, and the secret whisper of the soul in the heart, and for ever perceives the veils of mystery and the rainbows of hope upon our human horizons: which hears and sees, and yet turns wisely, meanwhile, to the life of the green earth, of which we are part, to the common kindred of living things, with which we are at one—is content, in a word, to live, because of the dream that makes living so mysteriously sweet and poignant; and to dream, because of the commanding immediacy of life.

As yet, of course, Alan and Ynys had known little of the vicissitudes of aroused life. What they did know, foresee, was due rather to the second-sight of the imagination than to the keen knowledge of experience.

In Alan, Ynys found all that her heart craved. She discovered this nearly too late. A year before this last home-coming of her cousin, she had been formally betrothed to Andrik de Morvan, the friend of her childhood, and for whom she had a true affection, and in that betrothal had been quietly glad. When, one midwinter day, she and Alan walked through an upland wood and looked across the snowy pastures and the white slopes beyond, all aglow with sunlight, and then suddenly turned towards each other, and saw in the eyes of each a wonderful light, and the next moment were heart to heart, it was all a revelation.

For long she did not realise what it meant. On that unforgettable day, when they had left the forest-ridge and were near Kerival again, she had sat for a time on one of the rude cattle-gates which are frequent in these woodlands, while Alan had leant beside her, looking up with eyes too eloquent, and speaking of what he dreamed, with sweet stammering speech of new-found love.

How she had struggled, mentally, with her duty, as she conceived it, towards Andrik. She was betrothed to him; he loved her; she loved him, too, although even already she realised that there is a love which is not only invincible and indestructible but that comes unsought, has no need for human conventions, is neither moral nor immoral, but simply all-potent and thenceforth sovereign. To yield to that may be wrong: but if so, it is wrong to yield to the call of hunger, the cry of thirst, the whisper of sleep, the breath of ill, the summons of death. It comes, and that

is all. The green earth may be another Endymion, and may dream that the cold moonshine
is all in all: but when the sun rises, and a new
heat and glory and passion of life are come, then
Endymion simply awakes.

It had been a sadness to her to have to tell
Andrik she no longer loved him as he was fain
to be loved. He would have no finality, then:
he held her to the bond—and in Brittany there
is a pledge akin to the 'hand-fast' of the north,
which makes a betrothal almost as binding as
marriage.

Andrik de Morvan had gone to the Marquis
de Kerival, and told him what Ynys had said.

'She is but a girl,' the Seigneur remarked
coldly. 'And you are wrong in thinking she
can be in love with any one else. There is no
one for whom she can care so much as for you:
no one whom she has met with whom she could
mate: no one with whom I would allow her to
mate.'

'But that matters little if she will not marry
me!' the young man had urged.

'My daughter is my daughter, de Morvan. I

cannot compel her to marry you. I know her
well enough to be sure that she would ignore
any command of this kind. But women are
fools: and one can get them to do what one
wants in one way if not in another. Let her be,
a while.'

'But the betrothal!'

'Let it stand. But do not press it. Indeed,
go away for a year. You are heir to your
mother's estates in Touraine. Go there: work:
learn all you can. Meanwhile, write occasionally
to Ynys. Do not address her as your betrothed,
but at the same time let her see that it is the
lover who writes. Then, after a few months,
confide that your absence is due solely to her:
that you cannot live without her: and that, after
a vain exile, you write to ask if you may come
and see her. They are all the same. It is the
same thing with my mares, for which Kerival is
so famous. Some are wild, some are docile, some
skittish, some vicious, some good, a few flawless
—but . . . well, they are all mares. One knows
a mare is not a sphinx. These complexities of
which we hear so much, what are they? Spin-

drift. The sea is simply the sea all the same.
The tide ebbs, though the poets reverse nature.
Ebb and flow, the lifting wind, the lifted wave:
we know the way of it all. It has its mystery,
its beauty; but we don't really expect to see a
nereid in the hollow of the wave, or to catch the
echo of a triton in the call of the wind. As for
Venus Anadyomene, the foam of which she was
made is the froth in poets' brains. Believe me,
Andrik, my friend, women are simply women:
creatures not yet wholly tamed, but tractable in
the main, delightful, valuable often, but certainly
not worth the tribute of passion and pain they
obtain from foolish men like yourself.'

With this worldly wisdom Andrik de Morvan
had gone home unconvinced. He loved Ynys:
and sophistries were an ineffectual balm.

But as for Ynys, she had long made up her
mind. Betrothal or no betrothal, she belonged
now only to one man, and that man Alan de
Kerival. She was his and his alone, by every
natural right. How could she help the accident
by which she had cared for Andrik before she
loved Alan? Now, indeed, it would be sacrilege

to be other than wholly Alan's. Was her heart not his, and her life with her heart, and with both her deathless devotion?

Alan, she knew, trusted her absolutely. Before he went back to Paris, after their love was no longer a secret, he had never once asked her to forfeit anything of her intimacy with Andrik, nor had he even urged the open cancelling of the betrothal. But, she was well aware, his own absolute loyalty involved for him a like loyalty from her: and she knew that forgiveness does not belong to those natures which stake all upon a single die.

And so the matter stood thus still. Ynys and Andrik de Morvan were nominally betrothed: and not only the Marquis and the Marquise de Kerival, but Andrik himself, looked upon the bond as absolute.

Perhaps Lois de Kerival was not without some suspicion as to how matters were between the betrothed pair. Certainly she knew that Ynys was not one who would give up any real or imagined happiness because of a conventional arrangement, or on account of any conventional duty.

In Alan, Ynys found all that he found in her. When she looked at him, she wondered how she could ever have dreamed of Andrik as a lover, for Alan was all that Andrik was not. How proud and glad she felt because of his great height and strength, his vivid features with their grey-blue eyes and *spirituel* expression, his wavy brown hair, a very type of youthful and beautiful manhood. Still more she revered and loved the inner Allan whom she knew so well, and recognised with a proud humility that this lover of hers, whom the great Daniel Darc had spoken of as a man of genius, was not only her knight, but her comrade, her mate, her ideal.

Often the peasants of Kerival had speculated if the young seigneur would join hands with her or with Annaik. Some hoped the one, some the other: but those who knew Alan otherwise than merely by sight felt certain that Ynys was the future bride.

'They are made for each other,' old Jeanne Mael, the village authority, was wont to exclaim; 'and the good God will bring them together soon or late. 'Tis a fair sweet couple they are: none

E

so handsome anywhere. That tall dark lass will be a good mother when her hour comes : an' the child o' him an' her should be the bonniest in the whole wide world.'

With that all who saw them together agreed.

CHAPTER V

I⸺ was an hour from midnight when Alan rose, opened a window, and looked out. The storm was over. He could see the stars glistening like silver fruit among the upper branches of the elms. Behind the great cypress known as the Fate of Kerival there was a golden radiance, as though a disc of radiant bronze were being slowly wheeled round and round, invisible itself, but casting a quivering gleam upon the fibrous undersides of the cypress-spires. Soon the moon would lift upward, and her paling gold become foam-white along the wide reaches of the forest.

The wind had suddenly fallen. In this abrupt lapse into silence there was something mysterious.

After so much violence, after that wild, tempestuous cry, such stillness ! There was no more than a faint rustling sound, as though invisible feet were stealthily flying along the pathway of the upper boughs, and through the dim defiles in the dense coverts of oak and beech in the very heart of the woods. Only, from hitherward of the unseen dunes, floated a melancholy sighing refrain, the echo of the eddying sea-breath among the pines. Beyond the last sands the deep hollow boom of the sea itself.

To stay indoors seemed to Alan a wanton forfeiture of beauty. The fragrance of the forest intoxicated him. Spring was come indeed. This wild storm had ruined nothing, for at its fiercest it had swept overhead : and on the morrow the virginal green world would be more beautiful than ever. Everywhere the green fire of Spring would be litten anew. A green flame would pass from meadow to hedgerow, from hedgerow to the tangled thickets of bramble and dog-rose, from the underwoods to the inmost forest glades. Everywhere song would be to the birds, everywhere young life would pulse, everywhere the rhythm of a new rapture would run rejoicing. The miracle of Spring would be

accomplished in the sight of all men, of all birds
and beasts, of all green life. Each in its kind
would have a swifter throb in the red blood or
the vivid sap.

No; he could not wait. No, Alan added to
himself with a smile, not even though to sleep
in the House of Kerival was to be beneath the
same roof as Ynys—to be but a few yards, a
passage, a corridor away. Ah, for sure, he could
dream his dream as well out there among the
gleaming boughs, in the golden sheen of the
moon, under the stars. Was there not the
silence for deep peace, and the voice of the
unseen sea for echo to the deep tides of love
which surged obscurely in his heart? Yes; he
would go out to that beautiful redemption of
the night. How often, in fevered Paris, he had
known that healing, either when his gaze was
held by the quiet stars, as he kept his hours-
long vigil, or when he escaped westward along
the banks of the Seine, and could wander undis-
turbed across grassy spaces or under shadowy
boughs.

In the great hall of the manor he found

white - haired Maticu asleep in his wicker
chair. The old man silently opened the heavy
oaken door, and with a smile, which somewhat
perplexed Alan, bowed to him as he passed
forth.

Could it be a space only of a few hours that
divided him from his recent arrival, he wondered.
The forest was no longer the same. Then it
was swept by the wind, lashed by the rains,
and was everywhere tortured into a tempestuous
music. Now it was so still, save for a ceaseless
faint dripping from wet leaves and the conduits
of a myriad sprays and branches, that he could
hear the occasional shaking of the wings of
hidden birds, ruffling out their plumage because of the moonlit quietudes that were come
again.

And then, too, he had seen Ynys : had held her
hand in his ; had looked in her beautiful hazel-
green eyes, dusky and wonderful as a starlit
gloaming because of the depth of her dear love ;
had pressed his lips to hers, and felt the throbbing of her heart against his own. There, in the
forest-edge, it was difficult to realise all this. It

would be time to turn soon, to walk back along the sycamore-margined Seine embankment, to reach the Tour de l'Ile and be at his post in the observatory again! Then he glanced backward, and saw a red light shining from the room where the Marquis de Kerival sat up late night after night, and he wondered if Ynys were still there, or if she were now in her room and asleep, or if she lay in a waking dream.

For a time he stared at this beacon. Then, troubled by many thoughts, but most by his love, he moved slowly into one of the beech-avenues which radiated from the fantastic medi-æval sundial at the end of the tulip-garden in front of the château.

While the moon slowly lifted from branch to branch, a transient stir of life came into the forest.

Here and there he heard low cries, sometimes breaking into abrupt eddies of arrested song: thrushes, he knew, ever swift to slide their music out against any tide of light. Once or twice a blackcap, in one of the beeches near the open, sang so poignantly a brief strain, that he thought

it that of a nightingale.   Later, in an oak-glade,
he heard the unmistakable song itself.

The sea-sound came hollowly under the boughs
like a spent billow.   Instinctively he turned that
way, and so crossed a wide glade that opened
on   the   cypress - alley   to   the   west   of   the
château.

Just as he emerged upon this glade he thought
he saw a stooping figure glide swiftly athwart the
northern end of it and disappear among the
cypresses.   Startled, he stood still.

No one stirred.   Nothing moved.   He could
hear no sound save the faint sighing of the wind-
eddy among the pines, the dull rhythmic beat
of the sea falling heavily upon the sands.

'It must have been a delusion,' he muttered.
Yet, for the moment, he had felt certain that the
crouching figure of a man had moved swiftly out
of the shadow of the solitary wide-spreading
thorn he knew so well, and had disappeared into
the darker shadow of the cypress-alley.

After all, what did it matter?   It could only
be some poor fellow poaching.   With a smile,
Alan remembered how often he had sinned like-

wise. He would listen, however, and give the
man a fright, for he knew that Tristran de
Kerival was stern in his resentment against
poachers, partly because he was liberal in certain
woodland-freedom he granted on the sole condition that none of the peasants ever came within
the home-domain.

Soon, however, he was convinced that he was
mistaken. Deep silence prevailed everywhere.
Almost, he fancied, he could hear the soft fall of
the dew. A low whirring sound showed that a
nightjar had already begun his summer-wooing.
Now that, as he knew from Ynys, the cuckoo was
come, and that the swallows had suddenly multi-
plied from a score of pioneers into a battalion
of ever-flying darts; now that he had listened
to the nightingales calling through the moonlit
woods, and had heard the love-note of the nightjar, the hot weather must be come at last—that
glorious tide of golden life which flows from
April to June, and makes them the joy of the
world.

Slowly he walked across the glade. At the old
thorn he stopped, and leaned awhile against its

rugged twisted bole, recalling incident after incident associated with it.

It was strangely restful there. Around him was the quiet sea of moonlight : yonder, behind the cypresses and the pine-crowned dunes, was the quiet sea of moving waters : yet, in the one, there was scarce less of silence than in the other. Ah, he remembered abruptly, on just such a night, years ago, he and Annaik had stood long there, hand in hand, listening to a nightingale. What a strange girl she was, even then. Well he recalled how, at the end of the song, and when the little brown singer had slipped from its bough like a stone slung from a sling, Annaik had laughed, though he knew not at what, and had all at once unfastened her hair, and let its tawny bronze-red mass fall about her shoulders. She was so beautiful and wild, that he had clasped her in his arms, and had kissed her again and again. And Annaik . . . oh, he remembered, half shyly, half exultantly . . . she had laughed again, but more low, and had tied the long drifts of her hair around his neck like a blood-red scarf.

It gave him a strange emotion to recall all this. Did Annaik also think of it ever, he wondered.

Then, too, had they not promised somewhat to each other? Yes. . . .

Annaik had said, 'One night we shall come here again, and then if you do not love me as much as you do now, I shall strangle you with my hair: and if you love me more we shall go away into the forest, and never return, or not for long, long: but if you do not love me at all, then you are to tell me so, and I will——'

'What?' he had asked, when she stopped abruptly.

At that, however, she had said no more as to what was in her mind, but had asked him to carve upon the thorn the 'A' of her name, and the 'A' of his, into a double 'A.' Yes, of course, he had done this: where was it, he pondered. Surely midway on the southward side, for then as now the moonlight would be there.

With an eagerness of which he was conscious he slipped from where he leaned, and examined the bole of the tree. A heavy branch intervened.

This he caught and withheld, and the light flooded upon the gnarled trunk.

With a start, Alan almost relinquished the branch. There, unmistakable, was a large carven ' A,' but not only was it the old double ' A ' made into a single letter, but clearly the change had been made quite recently, apparently within a few hours. Moreover, it was now linked to another letter. The legend ran : *A. & J.*

Puzzled, he looked close. There could be no mistake. The cutting was recent. The *J.*, indeed, might have been that moment done. Suddenly an idea flashed into his mind. He stooped and examined the mossed roots. Yes ; there were the fragments. He took one, and put it between his teeth : the wood was soft, and had the moisture of fibre recently severed.

Who was ' J.' ? Alan pondered over every name he could think of. He knew no one whose baptismal name began thus, with the exception of Jervaise de Morvan, the brother of Andrik, and he was married and resident in distant Pondicherry. Otherwise there was but Jak Bourzak, the woodcutter—a bent, broken-down old man, who could not have cut the letters for the good reason that he was unable to write, and was so ignorant that, even in that remote region, he was called Jak the Stupid. Alan was still pondering over this when suddenly the stillness was broken by the loud screaming of peacocks.

Kerival was famous for these birds, of which the peasantry stood in superstitious awe. Indeed, a legend was current to the effect that Tristran de Kerival maintained these resplendent creatures because they were the souls of his ancestors, or of such of them as before death had not been able to gain absolution for their sins. When they were heard crying harshly before rain or at sundown, or sometimes in the moonlight, the hearers shuddered. ' The lost souls of Kerival' became a saying, and there were prophets here and there who foreboded ill for Tristran the Silent, or some one near and dear to him, whenever that strange clamour rang forth unexpectedly.

Alan himself was surprised, startled. The night was so still, no further storm was imminent, and the moon had been risen for some time. Possibly the peacocks had strolled into the cypress-alley, to strut to and fro in the moonshine, as their wont was in the wooing-days, and two of them had come into jealous dispute.

Still, that continuous harsh tumult seemed rather to have the note of alarm than of quarrel. Alan walked to the seaward side of the thorn, but still kept within its shadow.

The noise was now not only clamant but startling. The savage screaming, like that of barbaric trumpets, filled the night.

Swiftly the listener crossed the glade, and was soon among the cypresses. There, while the dull thud of the falling seas was more than ever audible, and the screams of the peacocks were so insistent, that he had ears for these alone.

At the easter end of the alley the glade broke away into scattered pines, and from these swelled a series of low dunes. Alan could see them clearly from where he stood, under the boughs of a huge yew, one of several that grew here and there among their solemn columnar kin.

His gaze was upon this open space when,

abruptly, he started   A tall, slim figure, coming from the shore, moved slowly inland across the dunes.

Who could this walker in the dark be? The shadowy Walker in the Night herself, mayhap: the dreaded soulless woman who wanders at dead of night through forests, or by desolate shores, or by the banks of the perilous *marais*.

Often he had heard of her. When any man met this woman his fate depended on whether he saw her before she caught sight of him. If she saw him first, she had but to sing her wild strange song, and he would have to go to her; and when he was before her, two flames would come out of her eyes, and one flame would burn up his life as though it were dry tinder, and the other would wrap round his soul like a scarlet shawl, and she would take it and live with it in a cavern underground for a year and a day. And on that last day she would let it go, as a hare is let go a furlong beyond a greyhound. Then it would fly like a windy shadow from glade to glade, or from dune to dune, in the vain hope to reach a wayside Calvary: but ever in vain. Sometimes the Holy

Tree would almost be reached; then, with a gliding swiftness, like a flood racing down a valley, the Walker in the Night would be alongside the fugitive. Now and again unhappy night-farers—unhappy they, for sure, for never does weal remain with any one who hears what no human ear should hearken — would be startled by a sudden laughing in the darkness. This was when some such terrible chase had happened, and when the creature of the night had taken the captive soul, in the last moments of the last hour of the last day of its possible redemption, and rent it this way and that, as a hawk scatters the feathered fragments of its mutilated quarry.

Alan thought of this wild legend and shuddered. Years ago he had been foolhardy enough to wish to meet the phantom, to see her before she saw him, and to put a spell upon her. For, if this were possible, he could compel her to whisper some of her secret lore, and she could give him spells to keep him scatheless till old age.

But, as with fearful gaze he stared at the figure which so leisurely moved towards the cypress-alley, he was puzzled by some vague resemblance, by something familiar. The figure was that of a woman, unmistakably; and she moved as though she were in a dream.

But who could it be, there, in that lonely place, at that hour of the night? Who would venture or care . . .

In a flash all was clear. It was Annaik.

There was no room for doubt. He might have known her lithe walk, her wildwood grace, her peculiar carriage; but before recognition of these had come, he had caught a glimpse of her hair in the moonlight. It was like burnished brass in that yellow shine. There was no other such hair in the world, he believed.

But . . . Annaik! What could she be doing there? How had she been able to leave the château? When had she stolen forth? Where had she wandered? Whither was she going? To what end?

These and other thoughts stormed through Alan's mind. Almost, he muttered below his breath, almost he would rather have seen the Walker in the Night.

As she drew nearer he could see her as clearly

as though it were daylight.   She appeared to be thinking deeply, and ever and again to be murmuring disconnected phrases.   His heart smote him when he saw her twice raise her arms and then wring her hands, as if in sore straits of sorrow.

He did not stir.   He would wait, he thought. It might add to Annaik's strange grief, if grief it were, to betray his presence.   Again, was it possible that she was there to meet some one— to encounter the ' J.' whose initial was beside her own on the old thorn?   How pale she was, he noticed.   A few yards away her dress caught; she hesitated, slowly disengaged herself, but did not advance again.

For the third time she wrung her hands.

What could it mean?   Alan was about to move forward when he heard her voice.

' O Alan, Alan, Alan ! '

What . . . had she seen him?   He flushed there in the shadow, and words rose to his lips. Then he was silent, for she spoke again.

' I hate her . . . I hate her . . . not for herself, no, no, no . . . but because she has taken you from me.   Why does Ynys have you, all of you, when I have loved you all along? None of us knew anything—none, till last Noël. Then we knew; only neither you nor Ynys knew that I loved you as a soul in hell loves the memory of its earthly joy.'

Strange words, there in that place, at that hour; but far stranger the passionless voice in which the passionate words were uttered. Bewildered, Alan leaned forward intent. The words had waned to a whisper, but were now incoherent. Fragmentary phrases, irrelevant words, what could it all mean?

Suddenly an idea made him start. He moved slightly, so as to catch the full flood of a moonbeam as it fell on Annaik's face.

Yes, he was right. Her eyes were open, but were fixed in an unseeing stare. For the first time, too, he noted that she was clad simply in a long dressing-gown. Her feet were bare, and were glistening with the wet they had gathered; on her lustrous hair, nothing but the moonlight.

He had remembered. Both Annaik and Ynys had a tendency to somnambulism, a trait in-

herited from their father. It had been cured
years ago, he had understood. But here—here
was proof that Annaik, at any rate, was still
subject to that mysterious malady of sleep.

That she was absolutely trance-bound he saw
clearly. But what he should do—that puzzled,
that bewildered him.

Slowly Annaik, after a brief hesitancy when he
fancied she was about to awake, moved forward
again.

She came so close that almost she brushed
against him; would have done so, indeed, but
that he was hidden from contact as well as from
sight by the boughs of the yew, which on that
side swept to the ground.

Alan put out his hand. Then he withdrew it.
No, he thought, he would let her go unmolested,
and if possible unawaked; but he would follow
her, lest evil befell. She passed. His nerves
thrilled. What was this strange emotion that
gave him a sensation almost as though he had
seen his own wraith? But different . . . for,
oh! he could not wait to think about that, he
muttered.

He was about to stoop and emerge from the yew-boughs, when he heard a sound which made him stop abruptly.

It was a step; of that he felt sure. And at hand, too. The next moment he was glad he had not disclosed himself, for a crouching figure stealthily followed Annaik.

Surely that was the same figure he had seen cross the glade, the figure that had slipped from the thorn?

If so, could it be the person who had cut the letter ' J ' on the bark of the tree? The man kept so much in the shadow that it was difficult to obtain a glimpse of his 'face. Alan waited. In a second or two he would have to pass the yew.

Just before the mysterious pursuer reached the old tree, he stopped. Alan furtively glanced to his left. He saw that Annaik had suddenly halted. She stood intent, as though listening. Possibly she had awaked. He saw her lips move. She spoke, or called something: what, he could not hear because of the intermittent screaming of the peacocks.

When he looked at the man in the shadow he started. A moonbeam had penetrated the obscurity, and the face was white against the black background of a cypress.

Alan recognised the man in a moment. It was Jud Kerbastiou, the forester. What . . . was it possible: could *he* be the ' J ' who had linked his initial with that of Annaik ?

It was incredible. The man was not only a boor, but one with rather an ill repute. At any rate he was known to be a poacher as well as a woodlander of the old Breton kind—men who would never live save in the forest, any more than a gypsy would become a clerk and live in a street.

It was said among the peasants of Kerival that his father, old Iouenn Kerbastiou, the charcoal-burner, was an illegitimate brother of the late Marquis—so that Jud or Judik as he was generally called, was a blood-relation of the great folk at the château. Once this had been hinted to the Marquis Tristran. It was for the first and last time. Since then, Jud Kerbastiou had become more morose than ever, and was seldom seen among his fellows. When not with his infirm old father, at the hut in the woods that were to the eastward of the forest-hamlet of Ploumael, he was away in the densely wooded reaches to the south. Occasionally he was seen upon the slopes of the Black Hills, but this was only in winter, when he crossed over into Upper Brittany with a mule-train laden with cut fagots.

That he was prowling about the home-domain of Kerival was itself ominous : but that in this stealthy manner he should be following Annaik was to Alan a matter of genuine alarm. Surely the man could mean no evil against one of the Big House, and one, too, so much admired, and in a certain way loved, as Annaik de Kerival? And yet the stealthy movements of the peasant, his crouching gait, his patient dogging of her steps—and this, doubtless, ever since she had crossed the glade from the forest to the cypresses —all this had a menacing aspect.

At that moment the peacocks ceased their wild miaulling. Low and clear, Annaik's voice came thrillingly along the alley—

'Alan! Alan! O Alan, darling, are you there ?'

His heart beat.   Then a flush sprang to his
brow, as with sudden anger he heard Jud Kerbastiou, reply in a thick muffled tone—

'Yes, yes, . . . and, and I love you, Annaik !'

Possibly the sleeper heard and understood.
Even at that distance Alan saw the light upon
her face, the light from within.

Judik the peasant slowly advanced.   His
stealthy tread was light as that of a fox.   He
stopped when he was within a yard of Annaik.

'Annaik,' he muttered hoarsely, 'Annaik, it
was I who was out among the beeches in front of
the château while the storm was raging. Sure you
must have known it: else why would you come
out?   I love you, white woman.   I am only a
peasant . . . but I love you, Annaik de Kerival,
I love you—I love you—I love you !'

Surely she was on the verge of waking !   The
colour had come back to her white face, her lips
moved, as though stirred by a breath from within.
Her hands were clasped, and the fingers inter-
twisted restlessly.

Kerbastiou was so wrought that he did not

hear steps behind him as Alan moved swiftly forward.

'Sure, you will be mine at last,' the man cried hoarsely—'mine, and none to dispute . . . ay, and this very night, too.'

Slowly Jud put out an arm. His hand almost touched that of Annaik. Suddenly he was seized from behind, and a hand was clasped firmly upon his mouth. He did not see who his unexpected assailant was, but he heard the whisper that was against his ear:

'If you make a sound I will strangle you to death.'

With a nod, he showed that he understood.

'If I let go, for the moment, will you come back under the trees here where she cannot see or hear us?

Another nod.

Alan relaxed his hold, but did not wholly relinquish his grip. Kerbastiou turned and looked at him.

'Oh, it's *you*,' he muttered, as he followed his assailant into the shadow some yards back.

'Yes, Judik Kerbastiou; it is I, Alan de Kerival.'

'Well, what do you want?'

'What do I want? How dare you be so insolent, fellow!—you, who have been following a defenceless woman?'

'What have *you* been doing?'

'I . . . oh, of course I have been following Mademoiselle Annaik also . . . but that was . . . that was . . . to protect her.'

'And is it not possible I might follow her for the same reason?'

'It is not the same thing at all, Judik Kerbastiou, and you know it. In the first place, you have no right to be here at all. In the next, I am Mademoiselle Annaik's cousin, and——'

'And I am her lover.'

Alan stared at the man in sheer amaze. He spoke quietly and assuredly, nor seemed in the least degree perturbed.

'But . . . but . . . why, Kerbastiou, it is impossible!'

'What is impossible?'

'That Annaik could love *you*.'

'I did not say she loved me. I said I was her lover.'

'And you believe that you, a peasant, a man held in ill-repute even among your fellow-peasants, a homeless woodlander, can gain the love of the daughter of your Seigneur, of a woman nurtured as she has been?'

'You speak like a book, as the saying is, M. de Kerival.' Judik uttered the words mockingly, and with raised voice. Annaik, who was still standing as one entranced, heard it: for she whispered again, '*Alan! Alan! Alan!*'

'Hush, man, she will hear. Listen, Judik, I don't want to speak harshly. You know me. Every one here does. You must be well aware that I am the last person to despise you or any man because you are poor and unfortunate. But you *must* see that such a love as this of yours is madness.'

'All love is madness.'

'Oh, yes, of course. But, look you, Judik, what right have you to be here at all, in the home-domain, in the dead of night!'

'You love Ynys de Kerival.'

'Yes . . . well, yes, I do love her: but what then? What is that to you?'

'Well, I love Annaik. I am here by the same right as you are.'

'You forget. *I* am welcome. You come by stealth. Do you mean for a moment to say that you are here to meet Mademoiselle Annaik by appointment?'

The man was silent.

'Judik Kerbastiou!'

'Yes?'

'You are a coward. You followed this woman, whom you say you love, with intent to rob her.'

'You are a fool, Alan de Kerival.'

Alan raised his arm. Then, ashamed, he let it fall.

'Will you go? Will you go now, at once, or shall I wake Mademoiselle Annaik, and tell her what I have seen—and from what I believe I have saved her?'

'No, you need not wake her, nor tell her anything. I know she has never even given me a thought.'

Suddenly the man bowed his head. A sob burst through the dark.

Alan put his hand on his shoulder.

'Judik!'

'Judik Kerbastiou! I am sorry for you from my heart. But go . . . go now, at once. Nothing shall be said of this. No one shall know anything. If you wish me to tell my cousin, I will; then she can see you or not, as she may wish.'

'I go. But . . . yes, tell her. To-morrow. Tell her to-morrow. Only, I would not have hurt her. Tell her that. I go now. *Adiou.*'

With that, Judik Kerbastiou lifted his shaggy head, and turned his great, black, gypsy-wild eyes upon Alan.

'She loves *you*,' he said simply. Then he stepped lightly over the path, passed between the cypresses, and moved out across the glade. Alan watched his dark figure slide through the moonlight. He traversed the glade to the right of the thorn. For nearly half a mile he was visible; then he turned and entered the forest.

An hour later, two figures moved in absolute

silence, athwart the sand-dunes beyond the cypress-alley.

Hand in hand they moved. Their faces were in deep shadow, for the moonlight was now obscured by a league-long cloud.

When they emerged from the scattered pines to the seaward of the château, the sentinel peacocks saw them, and began once more their harsh barbaric screams.

The twain unclasped their hands, and walked steadily forward, speaking no word, not once looking one at the other.

As they entered the yew-close at the end of the old garden of the château, they were as shadows drowned in night. For some minutes, they were invisible, though, from above, the moon shone upon their white faces and on their frozen stillness. The peacocks sullenly ceased.

Once more they emerged into the moon dusk. As they neared the ivied gables of the west wing of the manor, the cloud drifted from the moon, and her white flood turned the obscurity into a radiance wherein every object stood forth as clear as at noon.

Alan's face was white as are the faces of the dead. His eyes did not once lift from the ground. But in Annaik's face was a flush, and her eyes were wild and beautiful as falling stars.

It was not an hour since she had wakened from her trance: not an hour, and yet already had Alan forgotten—forgotten her, and Ynys, and the storm, and the after-calm. Of one thing he thought only, and that was of what Daniel Darc had once said to him laughingly: ' If the old fables of astrology were true, your horoscope would foretell impossible things.'

In absolute silence they moved up the long flight of stone stairs that led to the château; in absolute silence they entered by the door which old Maticu had left ajar; in silence they passed that unconscious sleeper; in silence they crossed the landing where the corridors diverged.

Both stopped, simultaneously. Alan seemed about to speak, but his lips closed again without utterance.

Abruptly he turned. Without a word he passed along the corridor to the right, and disappeared in the obscurity

Annaik stood a while, motionless, silent. Then she put her hand to her heart. On her impassive face the moonlight revealed nothing: only in her eyes there was a gleam as of one glad unto death.

Then she too passed, noiseless and swift as a phantom. Outside, on the stone terrace, Ys, the blind peacock, strode to and fro, uttering his prolonged raucous screams. When, at last, he was unanswered by the peacocks in the cypress-alley, his clamant voice no longer tore the silence.

The moon trailed her flood of light across the earth. It lay upon the waters, and was still a glory there, when, through the chill quietudes of dawn, the stars waned one by one in the soft greying that filtered through the morning dusk. The new day was come.

CHAPTER VI

THE day that followed this quiet dawn marked the meridian of Spring. Thereafter the flush upon the blossoms would deepen—the yellow pass out of the green—and a deeper green involve the shoreless emerald sea of verdure which everywhere covered the brown earth, and swelled and lapsed in endlessly receding billows of forest and woodland. Up to that noontide height Spring had aspired, ever since she had shaken the dust of snow from her primrose-sandals : now, looking upon the way she had come, she took the hand of Summer—and both went forth as one, so that none should tell which was still the guest of the greenness.

This was the day when Alan and Ynys walked among the green alleys of the woods of Kerival,

G

and when, through the deep gladness that was
his, for all the strange gnawing pain in his mind,
in his ears echoed the haunting line of Rimbaud :
' Then, in the violet forest, all a-bourgeon,
Eucharis said to me : It is Spring.'

Through the first hours of the day Alan had
been unwontedly silent. Ynys had laughed at
him with loving eyes, but had not shown any
shadow of resentment. His word to the effect
that his journey had tired him, and that he had
not slept at all, was enough to account for his
lack of buoyant joy.

But, in truth, Ynys did not regret this, since it
had brought a still deeper intensity of love into
Alan's eyes. When he looked at her, there was
so much passion of longing, so pathetic an appeal,
that her heart smote her. Why should she be
the one chosen to evoke a love such as this, she
wondered : she, who was but Ynys, while Alan
was a man whom all women might love, and had
genius that made him as one set apart from his
fellows, and was brow-lit by a starry fate ?

And yet, in a sense, she understood. They
were so much at one, so like in all essential

matters, and were in all ways comrades. It would have been impossible for each not to love the other. But, deeper than this, was the profound and intimate communion of the spirit. In some beautiful strange way, she knew, she was the flame to his fire. At that flame he lit the torch of which Daniel Darc and others had spoken. She did not see why or wherein it was so, but she believed, and indeed at last realised the exquisite actuality.

In deep love, there is no height nor depth between two hearts, no height nor depth, no length nor breadth. There is simply love.

The birds of Angus Ogue are like the wild-doves of the forest: when they nest in the heart they are as one. And her life, and Alan's, were not these one ?

Nevertheless, Ynys was disappointed as the day went on, and her lover did not seem able to rouse himself from his strange despondency.

Doubtless this was due largely to what was pending. That afternoon he was to have his long anticipated interview with the Marquise, and would, perhaps, learn what might affect his

whole life. On the other hand, each believed
that nothing would be revealed which was not of
the past solely.

Idly, Ynys began to question her companion
about the previous night. What had he done,
since he had not slept : had he read, or dreamed
at the window, or gone out, as had once been his
wont on summer nights, to walk in the cypress-
alley or along the grassy dunes? Had he
heard a nightingale singing in the moonlight?
Had he noticed the prolonged screaming of the
peacocks—unusually prolonged, now that she
thought of it, Ynys added.

' I wonder, dear, if you would love me whatever
happened—whatever I was, or did ? '

It was an inconsequent question. She looked
up at him, half perturbed, half pleased.

' Yes, Alan.'

' But do you mean what you say, knowing that
you are not only using a phrase ? '

' I have no gift of expression, dearest. Words
come to me without their bloom and their
fragrance, I often think. But . . . Alan, *I love
you.*'

'That is sweetest music for me, Ynys, my fawn. All words from you have both bloom and fragrance, though you may not know it, shy flower. But tell me again, do you mean what you say, absolutely?'

'Absolutely. In every way, in all things, at all times. Dear, how could anything come between us? It is possible, of course, that circumstances might separate us: but nothing could really come between us. My heart is yours.'

'What about Andrik de Morvan?'

'Ah, you are not in earnest, Alan?'

'Yes; I am more than half in earnest, Ynys darling. Tell me!'

'You cannot possibly believe that I care, that I could care, for Andrik as I care for you, Alan.'

'Why not?'

'Why not? Oh, have you so little belief, then, in women, in me? Alan, do you not know that what is perhaps possible for a man, though I cannot conceive it, is *impossible* for a woman? That is the poorest sophistry which says a woman may love two men at the same time.

That is, if by love is meant what you and I mean. Affection, the deepest affection, is one thing: the love of man and woman, as we mean it, is a thing apart.'

'You love Andrik ?'

'Yes.'

'Could you wed your life with his ?'

'I could have done so . . . but for you.'

'Then, by your true heart, is there no possibility that he can in any way ever come between us ?'

'None.'

'Although he is nominally your betrothed, and believes in you as his future wife ?'

'That is not my fault. I drifted into that conditional union, as you know. But after to-day he and every one shall know that I can wed no man but you. But why do you ask me these things, Alan ?'

'I want to know. I will explain later. But tell me, could you be happy with Andrik? You say you love him ?'

'I love him, as a friend, as a comrade.'

'As an intimately dear comrade ?'

'Alan, do not let us misunderstand each other.

There can only be one supreme comrade for a woman : and that is the man whom she loves supremely. Every other affection, the closest, the dearest, is as distinct from that as day from night.'

'If by some malign chance you and Andrik married—say, in the event of my supposed death —would you still be as absolutely true to me as you are now ? '

'What has the accident of marriage to do with truth between a man and a woman, Alan ? '

'It involves intimacies that would be a desecration otherwise. O Ynys, do you not understand ? '

'It is a matter of the inner life. Men so rarely believe in the hidden loyalty of the heart. It is possible for a woman to fulfil a bond and yet not be a bondswoman. Outer circumstances have little to do with the inner life, with the real self.'

'In a word, then, if you married Andrik, you would remain absolutely mine, not only if I were dead, but if perchance the rumour were untrue, and I came back, though too late ? '

'Yes.'

'Absolutely?'

'Absolutely.'

'And you profoundly know, Ynys, that in no conceivable circumstances can Andrik be to you what I am, or anything for a moment approaching it?'

'I do know it.'

'Although he were your husband?'

'Although he were my husband.'

The worn lines that were in Alan's face were almost gone. Looking into his eyes, Ynys saw that the strange look of pain which had alarmed her was no longer there. The dear eyes had brightened: a new hope seemed to have arisen in them.

'Do you believe me, Alan dear?' she whispered.

'If I did not, it would kill me, Ynys.'

And he spoke truth. The bitter sophistications of love play lightly with the possibilities of death. Men who talk of suicide are likely to be long-livers : lovers whose hearts are easily broken can generally recover and astonish themselves by their heroic endurance. The human heart is like a wave of the sea: it can be lashed into storm, it can be calmed, it can become stagnant —but it is seldom absorbed from the ocean till in natural course the sun takes up its spirit in vapour. Yet, ever and again, there is one wave among a myriad which a spiral wind-eddy may suddenly strike. In a moment it is whirled this way and that: it is involved in a cataclysm of waters: and then cloud and sea meet, and what a moment before had been an ocean-wave is become an idle skiey vapour.

Alan was of the few men of whom that wave is the symbol. To him death could come at any time, if the wind-eddy of a certain unthinkable sorrow struck him at his heart.

In this sense, his life was in Ynys' hands as absolutely as though he were a caged bird. He knew it, and Ynys knew it.

There are a few men, a few women, like this. Perhaps it is well that these are so rare. Among the hills of the north, at least, they may still be found: in remote mountain-valleys and in lonely isles, where life and death are realised actualities and not the mere adumbrations of the pinions of

that lonely fugitive, the human mind, along the
endless precipices of Time.

Alan knew well that both he and Ynys were
not so strong as each believed. Knowing this,
he feared for both. And yet, there was but one
woman in the world for him—Ynys: as, for her,
there was but one man—Alan.

Without her he could do nothing, achieve
nothing. She was his flame, his inspiration, his
strength, his light. Without her he was afraid
to live: with her, death was a beautiful dream.
To her, Alan was not less. She lived in and for
him.

But we are wrought of marsh-fire as well as of
stellar light. Now, as of old, the gods do not
make of the fairest life a thornless rose. A
single thorn may innocently convey poison: so
that everywhere men and women go to and fro
perilously, and not least those who move through
the shadow and shine of an imperious passion.

For a time, thereafter, Alan and Ynys walked
slowly onward, hand in hand, each brooding
deep over the thoughts their words had stirred.

'Do you know what Yann says, Alan?' Ynys
asked, in a low voice, after both had stopped
instinctively to listen to a thrush leisurely iterat-
ing his just learned love-carol, where he swung
on a greening spray of honeysuckle, under a
yellow-green lime.

'Do you know what Yann says? . . . He says
that you have a wave at your feet. What does
that mean?'

'When did he tell you that, Ynys mo-chree?'

'Ah, Alan, dear, how sweet it is to hear from
your lips the dear Gaelic we both love so well.
And does that not make you more than ever
anxious to learn all that you are to hear this
afternoon?'

'Yes . . . but that, that Ian Macdonald said :
what else did he say?'

'Nothing. He would say no more. I asked
him in the Gaelic, and he repeated only, "I see
a wave at his feet."'

'What Ian means by that I know well. It
means I am going on a far journey.'

'Oh, no, Alan, no !'

'He has the sight upon him, at times. Ian

would not say that thing, did he not mean it.
Tell me, my fawn, has he ever said anything of
this kind about *you*?'

'Yes. Less than a month ago. I was with
him one day on the dunes near the sea. Once,
when he gave no answer to what I asked, I looked
at him, and saw his eyes fixed. "What do you
see, Yann?" I asked.

'"I see great rocks, strange caverns. Sure,
it is well I am knowing what they are. They
are the sea-caves of Rona."

'There were no rocks visible from where we
stood, so I knew that Ian was in one of his
visionary moods. I waited, and then spoke
again, whisperingly—

'"Tell me, Ian MacIain, what do you see?"

'"I see two whom I do not know. And they
are in a strange place, they are. And on the
man I see a shadow, and on the woman I see a
light. But what that shadow is I do not know:
nor do I know what that light is. But I am for
thinking that it is of the Virgin Mary, for I see
the dream that is in the woman's heart, and it is
a fair wonderful dream *that*."

'That is all Yann said, Alan. As I was about to speak his face changed.

'"What is it, Ian?" I asked.

'At first he would answer nothing. Then he said, "It is a dream; it means nothing. It was only because I was thinking of you and Alan MacAlasdair."'

'O Ynys,' Alan interrupted, with an eager cry, 'that is a thing I have long striven to know : that which lies in the words " Alan MacAlasdair." My father, then, was named Alasdair! And was it Rona, you said, was the place of the sea-caves? Rona . . . that must be an island. The only Rona I know of is that near Skye. It may be the same. Now, indeed, I have a clue, lest I should learn nothing to-day. Did Ian say nothing more?'

'Nothing. I asked him if the man and woman he saw were you and I, but he would not speak. I am certain he was about to say yes, but refrained.'

For a while they walked on in silence, each revolving many speculations aroused by the clue given by the words of ' Yann the Dumb.' Suddenly Ynys tightened her clasp of Alan's hand.

'What is it, dear?'

'Alan, some time ago you asked me abruptly what I knew about the forester, Judik Kerbastiou. Well, I see him in that beech-covert yonder, looking at us.'

Alan started. Ynys noticed that for a moment he grew pale as foam. His lips parted, as though he were about to call to the woodlander : when Judik advanced, making at the same time a sign of silence.

The man had a wild look about him. Clearly he had not slept since he and Alan had parted at midnight. His dusky eyes had a red light in them. His rough clothes were still damp; his face, too, was strangely white and dank.

Alan presumed that he came to say something concerning Annaik. He did not know what to do to prevent this; but, while he was pondering, Judik spoke, in a hoarse, tired voice—

'Let the Lady Ynys go back to the château at once. She is needed there.'

'Why, what is wrong, Judik Kerbastiou?'

'Let her go back, I say. No time for words now.
Be quick. I am not deceiving you. Listen . . .'
and with that he leaned towards Alan, and whispered in his ear.

Alan looked at him in startled amaze. Then,
turning towards Ynys, he asked her to go back
at once to the château.

CHAPTER VII

'DEIREADH GACH COGAIDH, SITH'
('The end of all warfare, Peace')

ALAN did not wait till Ynys was out of sight,
before he demanded the reason of Judik's strange
appearance and stranger summons.

'Why are you here again, Judik Kerbastiou?
What is the meaning of this haunting of the
forbidden home-domain? And what did you
mean by urging Mademoiselle Ynys to go back
at once to the château?'

'Time enough later for your other questions,
young sir. Meanwhile, come along with me, and
as quick as you can.'

Without another word the woodlander turned
and moved rapidly along a narrow path through
the brushwood.

Alan saw it would be useless to ask further

questions at the moment; moreover, he was now vaguely alarmed. What could all this mystery mean ? Could an accident have happened to the Marquis Tristran ? It was hardly likely, for he seldom ventured into the forest, unless when the weather had dried all the ways : for he had to be wheeled in his chair, and, as Alan knew, disliked to leave the gardens or the well-kept yew and cypress-alleys near the château.

In a brief while, however, he heard voices. Judik turned, and waved to him to be wary. The forester bent forward, stared intently, and then beckoned to Alan to creep up alongside.

' Who is it ? What is it, Judik ? '

' Look.'

Alan disparted a bough of underwood which made an effectual screen. In the glade beyond were four figures.

One of these he recognised at once. It was the Marquis de Kerival. He was, as usual seated in his wheeled chair. Behind him, some paces to the right, was Raif Kermorvan, the steward of Kerival. The other two men Alan had not seen before.

One of these strangers was a tall, handsome
man, of about sixty.   His close-cropped white
hair, his dress, his whole mien, betrayed the
military man.   Evidently a colonel, Alan thought.
or perhaps a general : at any rate an officer of
high rank, and one to whom command and self-
possession were alike habitual.

Behind this gentleman, one of the most distinguished and even noble-looking men he had
ever seen, and again some paces to the right,
was a man, evidently a groom, and to all appearances an orderly in mufti.

The first glance revealed that a duel was
imminent.   The duellists, of course, were the
military stranger and the Marquis de Kerival.

'Who is that man?' Alan whispered to
Kerbastiou.   'Do you know ?.'

'I do not know his name.   He is a soldier—
a general.   He came to Kerival to-day : an hour
or more ago.   I guided him through the wood,
for he and his man had ridden into one of the
winding alleys and had lost their way.   I heard
him ask for the Marquis de Kerival.   I waited
about in the shrubbery of the rose-garden to see

if . . . if . . . some one for whom I waited . . .
would come out. After a time, half an hour or
less, this gentleman came forth, ushered by Raif
Kermorvan the steward. His man brought
around the two horses again. They mounted,
and rode slowly away. I joined them, and offered
to show them a shorter route than that which
they were taking. The general said they wished
to find a glade known as Merlin's Rest. Then
I knew what he came for, I knew what was
going to happen.'

' What, Judik ? '

' Hush, not so loud ! They will hear us ! I
knew it was for a duel. It was here that Andrik
de Morvan, the uncle of him whom you know,
was killed by a man—I forget his name.'

' Why did the man kill Andrik de Morvan ? '

' Oh, who knows ? Why does one kill anybody ?
Because he was tired of enduring the Sieur
Andrik longer : he bored him beyond words to
tell, I have heard. Then, too, the Count, for
he was a Count, loved Andrik's wife.'

Alan glanced at Judik. For all his rough wildness, he spoke on occasion like a man of breed-

ing. Moreover, at no time was he subservient
in his manner. Possibly, Alan thought, it was
true what he had heard: that Judik Kerbastiou
was by moral right Judik de Kerival.

While the onlookers were whispering, the four
men in the glade had all slightly shifted their
position. The Marquis, it was clear, had insisted
upon this. The light had been in his eyes. Now
the antagonists and their seconds were arranged
aright. Kermorvan, the steward, was speaking
slowly: directions as to the moment when to fire.

Alan knew it would be worse than useless to
interfere. He could but hope that this was no
more than an affair of honour of a kind not
meant to have a fatal issue ; a political quarrel,
perhaps : a matter of insignificant social offence.

Before Raif Kermorvan—a short, black-haired,
bull-necked man, with a pale face and protrud-
ing light-blue eyes—had finished what he had
to say, Alan noticed what had hitherto escaped
him : that immediately beyond the glade, and
under a huge sycamore already in full leaf, stood
the Kerival carriage. Alain the coachman sat
on the box, and held the two black horses in

rein. Standing by the side of the carriage was Georges de Rohan, the doctor of Kerloek, and a personal friend of the Marquis Tristran.

Suddenly Kermorvan raised his voice.

' M. le Général, are you ready ? '

' I am ready,' answered a low, clear voice.

' M. le Marquis, are you ready ? '

Tristran de Kerival did not answer, but assented by a slight nod.

' Then raise your weapons, and fire the moment I say " thrice." '

Both men raised their pistols.

' You have the advantage of me, sir,' said the Marquis coldly, in a voice as audible to Alan and Judik as to the others. ' I present a good aim to you here. Nevertheless, I warn you once more that you will not escape me . . . this time.'

The general smiled, scornfully Alan thought. Again, when suddenly he lowered his pistol and spoke, Alan fancied he detected if not a foreign accent, at least a foreign intonation.

' Once more, Tristran de Kerival, I tell you that this duel is a crime ; a crime against me ;

a crime against Madame la Marquise; a crime against your daughters; and a crime against——'

'That will do, General. I am ready. Are you?'

Without further word the stranger slowly drew himself together. He raised his arm, while his opponent did the same.

'*Once!*'

'*Twice!*'

'*Thrice!*'

There was a crack like that of a cattle-whip. Simultaneously some splinters of wood were blown from the left side of the wheeled-chair.

The Marquis Tristran smiled. He had reserved his fire. He could aim now with fatal effect.

'It is murder,' muttered Alan, horrified: but at that moment the Marquis spoke. Alan leaned forward intent to hear.

'*At last.*' That was all. But in the words was a concentrated longing for revenge, the utterance of a vivid hate.

Tristran de Kerival slowly and with methodical malignity took aim. There was a flash, the same whip-like crack.

For a moment it seemed as though the ball had missed its mark. Then suddenly there was a bubbling of red froth at the mouth of the stranger. Still, he stood erect.

Alan looked at the Marquis de Kerival. He was leaning back, deathly white, but with the bitter suppressed smile which every one at the château knew and hated.

All at once, the general swayed, lunged forward, and fell prone.

Dr. de Rohan ran out from the sycamore, and knelt beside him. After a few seconds he looked up.

He did not speak, but every one knew what his eyes said. To make it unmistakable, he drew out his handkerchief and put it over the face of the dead man.

Alan was about to advance when Judik Kerbastiou plucked him by the sleeve.

'Hist! M'sieur Alan! There is Mamzell Ynys returning! She will be here in another minute. She must not see what is there.'

'You are right, Judik. I thank you.'

With that, he turned and moved swiftly down

the leaf-hid path which would enable him to intercept Ynys.

' What is it, Alan ?' she asked, with wondering eyes, the moment he was at her side. ' What is it ?   Why are you so pale ? '

'It is because of a duel that has been fought here.   You must go back at once, dear.   There are reasons why you——'

' Is my father one of the combatants ?   I know he is out of the château.   Tell me, quick !   Is he wounded ?   Is he dead ? '

' No, no, darling heart.   He is unhurt.   But I can tell you nothing more just now.   Later . . . later.   But why did you return here ? '

'I came with a message from my mother. She is in sore trouble, I fear.   I found her, on her couch in the Blue Salon, with tears streaming down her face, and sobs choking her.'

' And she wants me . . . now ? '

' Yes.   She told me to look for you, and bring you to her at once.'

' Then go straightway back, dear, and tell her that I shall be with her immediately.   Yes, go— go—at once.'

But by the time Ynys had moved into the alley which led her to the château, and Alan had returned to the spot where he had left Judik, rapid changes had occurred.

The wheeled-chair had gone. Alan could see it nearing the South Yews: with the Marquis Tristran in it, leaning backward and with head erect. At its side walked Raif Kermorvan. He seemed to be whispering to the Seigneur. The carriage had disappeared: with it Georges de Rohan, the soldier-orderly, and, presumably, the dead man.

Alan stood hesitant, uncertain whether to go first to the Marquise, or to follow the man whom he regarded now with an aversion infinitely deeper than he had ever done hitherto; with whom, he felt, he never wished to speak again, for he was a murderer, if ever man was, and, from Alan's standpoint, a coward as well. Tristran de Kerival was the deadliest shot in all the country-side, and he must have known that when he challenged his victim he gave him his death-sentence.

It did not occur to Alan that possibly the

survivor was the man challenged. Instinctively he knew that this was not so.

Judik suddenly touched his arm.

' Here,' he said, ' this is the name of the dead man. I got the servant to write it down for me.'

Alan took the slip of paper. On it was, *M. le Général Carmichael.*

CHAPTER VIII

WHEN Alan reached the château he was at once accosted by old Matieu.

'Madame la Marquise wishes to see you in her private room, M'sieu Alan, and without a moment's delay.'

In a few seconds he was on the upper landing. At the door of the room known as the Blue Salon he met Yann the Dumb.

'What is it, Ian? Is there anything wrong?'

In his haste he spoke in French. The old islander looked at him, but did not answer.

Alan repeated his question in Gaelic.

'Yes, Alan MacAlasdair, I fear there is gloom and darkness upon us all.'

'Why?'

'By this an' by that. But I have seen the

death-cloth about Lois nic Alasdair bronnach
for weeks past. I saw it about her feet, and
then about her knees, and then about her breast.
Last night, when I looked at her, I saw it at her
neck. And to-day, the shadow-shroud is risen
to her eyes.'

'But your second-sight is not always true, you
know, Ian. Why, you told me when I was here
last that I would soon be seeing my long-dead
father again, and, more than that, that I should
see him but he never see me. But of this and
your other dark sayings, no more now. Can I
go in at once and see my aunt ? '

'I will be asking that, Alan-mo-caraid. But
what you say is not true. I have never yet " seen "
anything that has not come to pass : though
I have had the sight but seldom, to Himself
be the praise.' With that Ian entered, exchanged
a word or two, and ushered Alan into the room.

On a couch beside a great fireplace, across the
iron brazier of which were flaming pine-logs, an
elderly woman lay almost supine. That she had
been a woman of great beauty was unmistakable,
for all her grey hair and the ravages that time

and suffering had wrought upon her face. Even now her face was beautiful : mainly from the expression of the passionate dusky eyes which were so like those of Annaik. Her long inert body was covered with a fantastic Italian silk-cloth, whose gay pattern emphasised her own helpless condition. Alan had not seen her for some months, and he was shocked at the change. Below the eyes, as flamelike as ever, were purplish shadows, and everywhere through the habitual ivory of the delicate features a grey ashiness had diffused. When she held out her hand to him, he saw it as transparent as a fan, and perceived within it the red gleam of the fire.

'Ah, Alan, it is you at last! How glad I am to see you!' The voice was one of singular sweetness, in tone and accent much like that of Ynys.

'Dear Aunt Lois, not more glad than I am to see you,'—and, as he spoke, Alan kneeled at the couch and kissed the frail hand that had been held out to him.

'I would have so eagerly seen you at once on my arrival,' he resumed, 'but I was given your

message : that you had one of your seasons of
suffering, and could not see me.   You have been
in pain, Aunt Lois ? '

'Yes, dear, I am dying.'

'Dying !   Oh, no, no, no.   You don't mean
that.   And besides——'

'Why should I not mean it ?   Why should I
fear it, Alan ?   Has life meant so much to me of
late years that I should wish to prolong it ?'

'But you have endured so long ! '

'A bitter reason, truly ! . . . and one too apt
to a woman !   Well, enough of this.   Alan, I
want to speak to you about yourself.   But first
tell me one thing.   Do you love any woman ? '

'Yes, with all my heart, with all my life, I
love a woman.'

'Have you told her so ?   Has she betrothed
herself to you ? '

'Yes.'

'Is it Annaik ? '

'Annaik . . . Annaik ! '

'Why are you so surprised, Alan ?   Annaik is
beautiful : she has long loved you, I am certain :
and you, too, if I mistake not, care for her ? '

'Of course I do: of course I care for her, Aunt Lois, I love her. But I do not love her as you mean.'

The Marquise looked at him steadily.

'I do not quite understand,' she said gravely. 'I must speak to you about Annaik, later. But now, will you tell me who the woman is?'

'Yes. It is Ynys.'

'Ynys! But, Alan, do you not know that she is betrothed to Andrik de Morvan?'

'I know.'

'And that such a betrothal is, in Brittany, almost as binding as a marriage?'

'I have heard that said.'

'And that the Marquis de Kerival wishes the union to take place?'

'The Marquis Tristran's opinion on any matter does not in any way concern me.'

'That may be, Alan. But it concerns Ynys. Do you know that I also wish her to marry Andrik: that his parents wish it; and that every one regards the union as all but an accomplished fact?'

'Yes, dear Aunt Lois, I have known or presumed all you tell me. But nothing of it can alter what is a vital part of my existence.'

'Do you know that Ynys herself gave her pledge to Andrik de Morvan?'

'It was a conditional pledge. But in any case she will formally renounce it.'

For a time there was silence.

Alan had risen, and now stood by the side of the couch with folded arms. The Marquise Lois looked up at him with her steadfast shadowy eyes. When she spoke again she averted them, and her voice was so low as almost to be a whisper.

'Finally, Alan, let me ask you one question. It is not about you and Ynys. I infer that both of you are at one in your determination to take everything into your own hands. Presumably you can maintain her and yourself. Tristran— the Marquis de Kerival—will not contribute a franc towards her support. If he knew, he would turn her out of doors this very day.'

'Well, Aunt Lois, I wait for your final question?'

'It is this. *What about Annaik?*'

Startled by her tone and sudden lifted glance,

Alan stared in silence : then recollecting himself, he repeated dully—

'What about Annaik? . . . Annaik, Aunt Lois, why do you ask me about Annaik?'

'She loves you.'

'As a brother; as the betrothed of Ynys; as a dear comrade and friend.'

'Do not be a hypocrite, Alan. You know that she loves you. What of your feeling towards her?'

'I love her . . . as a brother loves a sister . . . as any old playmate and friend . . . as . . . as the sister of Ynys.'

A faint scornful smile came upon the white lips of the Marquise.

'Will you be good enough, then, to explain about last night.'

'About last night?'

'Come, be done with evasion. Yes, about last night. Alan, I know that you and Annaik were out together in the cypress-avenue, and again on the dunes, after midnight; that you were seen walking hand in hand; and that, stealthily, you entered the house together.'

I

' Well ? '

' Well !   The inference is obvious.   But I will
let you see that I know more.   Annaik went out
of the house late.   Old Matieu let her out.
Shortly after that you went out of the château.
Later, you and she came upon Judik Kerbastiou
prowling about in the woods.   It was more than
an hour after he left you that you returned to
the château.   Where were you during that hour
or more ? '

Alan flushed.   He unfolded his arms, hesitated,
then refolded them.

' How do you know this ? ' he asked simply.

' I know it, because——'

But before she finished what she was about to
say, the door opened and Yann entered.

' What is it, Ian ? '

' I would be speaking to you alone for a minute,
Bantighearna.'

' Alan, go to the alcove yonder, please.   I
must hear in private what Yann has to say to
me.'

As soon as the young man was out of hearing,
Yann stooped and spoke in low tones.   The

Marquise Lois grew whiter and whiter till not a vestige of colour remained in her face, and the only sign of life was in the eyes. Suddenly she made an exclamation.

Alan turned and looked at her. He caught her agonised whisper: '*O my God!*'

'What is it, oh, what is it, dear Aunt Lois?' he cried, as he advanced to her side.

He expected to be waved back, but to his surprise the Marquise made no sign to him to withdraw. Instead, she whispered some instructions to Yann and then bade him go.

When they were alone once more, she took a small silver flagon from beneath her coverlet and poured a few drops upon some sugar. Having taken this she seemed to breathe more easily. It was evident, at the same time, that she had received some terrible shock.

'Alan, come closer. I cannot speak loud. I have no time to say more to you about Annaik. I must leave that to you and to her. But lest I die, let me say at once that I forbid you to marry Ynys, and that I enjoin you to marry Annaik, and that without delay.'

A spasm of pain crossed the speaker's face. She stopped and gasped for breath. When at last she resumed, it was clear she considered as settled the matter on which she had spoken.

'Alan, I am so unwell that I must be very brief. And now listen. You are twenty-five to-day. Such small fortune as is yours comes now into your possession. It has been administered for you by a firm of lawyers in Edinburgh. See, here is the address. Can you read it? Yes? . . . well, keep the slip. This fortune is not much; to many, possibly to you, it may not seem enough to provide more than the bare necessities of life, not enough for its needs. Nevertheless, it is your own, and you will be glad. It will, at least, suffice. to keep you free from need if ever you fulfil your great wish to go back to the land of your fathers, to your own place.'

'That is still my wish and my hope.'

'So be it. You will have also an old sea-castle, not much more than a keep, on a remote island. It will at any rate be your own.

It is on an island where few people are, a wild
and precipitous isle far out in the Atlantic at
the extreme of the Southern Hebrides.'

'Is it called Rona?' Alan interrupted eagerly.

Without noticing or heeding his eagerness, she
assented.

'Yes, it is called Rona. Near it are the isles
of Mingulay and Borosay. These three islands
were once populous, and it was there that for
hundreds of years your father's clan, of which
he was hereditary chief, lived and prospered
After the evil days, the days when the young
king was hunted in the west as though a royal
head were the world's desire, and when our brave
kinswoman, Flora Macdonald, proved that women
as well as men could dare all for a good cause—
after those evil days the people melted away.
Soon the last remaining handful were upon
Borosay; and there, too, till the great fire that
swept the island a score of years ago, stood
the castle of my ancestors, the Macdonalds of
Borosay.

'My father was a man well known in his day.
The name of Sir Kenneth Macdonald was as

familiar in London as in Edinburgh, and in Paris
he was known to all the military and diplomatic
world, for in his youth he had served in the
French army with distinction, and held the
honorary rank of general.

'Not long before my mother's death he came
back to our lonely home in Borosay, bringing
with him a kinsman of another surname, who
owned the old castle of Rona on the Isle of the
Sea-Caves, as Rona is often called by the people
of the Hebrides. Also there came with him a
young French officer of high rank. After a time
I was asked to marry this man. I did not love
him, did not even care for him, and I refused. In
truth . . . already, though unknowingly, I loved
your father, he that was our kinsman and owned
Rona and its old castle. But Alasdair did not
speak; and because of that we each came to
sorrow.

'My father told me he was ruined. If I did
not marry Tristran de Kerival, he would lose all.
Moreover, my dying mother begged me to save
the man she had loved so well and truly, though
he had left her so much alone.

'Well, to be brief, I agreed. My kinsman Alasdair was away at the time. He returned on the eve of the very day on which I was suddenly married by Father Somerled Macdonald. We were to remain a few weeks in Borosay because of my mother's health.

'When Alasdair learned what had happened, he was furious. I believe he even drew a riding-whip across the face of Tristran de Kerival. Fierce words passed between them, and a cruel taunt that rankled. Nor would Alasdair have any word with me at all. He sent me a bitter message, but the bitterest word he could send was that which came to me : that he and my sister Silis had gone away together.

'From that day, I never saw Silis again, till the time of her death. Soon afterwards our mother died, and while the island-funeral was being arranged, our father had a stroke, and himself died, in time to be buried along with his wife. It was only then that I realised how more than true had been his statements as to his ruin. He died penniless. I was reminded of this unpleasant fact at the time, by the Marquis

de Kerival; and I have had ample opportunity
since for bearing it in vivid remembrance.

'As soon as possible we settled all that could
be settled, and left for Brittany. I have sometimes thought my husband's love was killed when
he discovered that Alasdair had loved me. He
forbade me even to mention his name, unless he
introduced it: and he was wont to swear that a
day would come when he would repay in full
what he believed to be the damning insult he
had received.

' We took with us only one person from Borosay,
an islander of Rona. He is, in fact, a clansman
both of you and me. It is of Ian I speak, of
course, him that soon came to be called here
Yann the Dumb. My husband and I had at
least this to unite us: that we were both Celtic,
and had all our racial sympathies in common.

'I heard from Silis that she was married, and
was happy. I am afraid this did not add to
my happiness. She wrote to me, too, when she
was about to bear her child. Strangely enough,
Alasdair, who, like his father before him, was an
officer in the French army, was then stationed

not far from Kerival, though my husband knew
nothing of this at first. My own boy and Silis's
were born about the same time. My child died:
that of Silis and Alasdair lived. You are that
child. No . . . wait, Alan . . . I will tell you
his name shortly. . . . You, I say, are that child.
Soon afterwards, Silis had a dangerous relapse.
In her delirium she said some wild things : among
them, words to the effect that the child which
had died was hers, and that the survivor was
mine—that, somehow or other, they had been
changed. Then, too, she cried out in her way-
wardness—and, poor girl, she must have known
then that Alasdair had loved me before he loved
her—that the child who lived, he who had been
christened Alan, was the child of Alasdair and
myself.

'All this poor delirium at the gate of death
meant nothing. But in some way it came to
Tristran's ears, and he believed. After Silis's
death I had brought you home, Alan, and had
announced that I would adopt you. I promised
Silis this, in her last hour, when she was in
her right mind again: also that the child, you,

should be brought up to speak and think in our own ancient language, and that in all ways you should grow up a true Gael. I have done my best, Alan ? '

'Indeed, indeed you have. I shall never, never forget that you have been my mother to me.'

'Well, my husband never forgave that. He acquiesced, but he never forgave. For long, and I fear to this day, he persists in his belief that you are really my illegitimate child, and that Silis was right in thinking that I had succeeded in having my own new-born babe transferred to her arms, while her dead offspring was brought to me, and, as my own, interred. It has created a bitter feud, and that is why he hates the sight of you. That, too, Alan, is why he would never consent to your marriage with either Ynys or Annaik.'

'But you yourself urged me a little ago to . . . to . . . marry Annaik.'

'I had a special reason. Besides, I of course know the truth. In his heart, God knows, my husband cannot doubt it.'

'Then tell me this: is my father dead also, as I have long surmised?'

'No . . . yes, yes, Alan, he is dead.'

Alan noticed his aunt's confusion, and regarded her steadily.

'Why do you first say "no" and then "yes."'

'Because——'

But here again an interruption occurred. The portière moved back, and then the wide doors disparted. Into the Salon was wheeled a chair, in which sat the Marquis de Kerival. Behind him was his attendant: at his side, Kermorvan the steward. The face of the Seigneur was still deathly pale, and the features were curiously drawn. The silky hair, too, seemed whiter than ever, and white as foam-drift on a dark wave were the long thin hands which lay on the lap of the black velvet shooting-jacket he wore.

'Ah, Lois, is this a prepared scene?' he exclaimed, in a cold and sneering voice, 'or has the young man known all along?'

'Tristran, I have not yet told him what I now know. Be merciful.'

'Alan MacAlasdair, as the Marquise here

calls you—and she ought to know—have you
learned yet the name and rank of your father?'

'No.'

'Tell him, Lois.'

'Tristran, listen. All is over now. Soon I
too shall be gone. In the name of God I pray
you to relent from this long cruelty, this remorse-
less infamy. You know as well as I do that our
first-born is dead twenty-five years ago, and that
this man here is truly the son of Silis, my sister.
And here is one overwhelming proof for you : I
have just been urging him to marry Annaik.'

At that Tristran the Silent was no longer
silent. With a fierce laugh he turned to the
steward—

'I call you to witness, Raif Kermorvan, that
I would kill Annaik, or Ynys either for that
matter, before I would allow such an unnatural
union. Once and for all I absolutely ban it.
Besides . . . Listen, you there with your father's
eyes! You are sufficiently a Gael to feel that
you would not marry the daughter of a man who
killed your father ?'

'God forbid!'

'Well, then, God does forbid.   Lois, tell this
man what you know.'

'Alan,' began the Marquise quaveringly, her
voice fluttering like a dying bird, 'the name
of your father is . . . is . . . Alasdair . . .
Alasdair Carmichael!'

'*Carmichael!*'

For a moment he was dazed, bewildered.
When, recently, had he heard that name ?

Then it flashed upon him.   He turned with
flaming eyes to where the Marquis sat, quietly
watching him.

'O my God!'   That was all.   He could say
no more.   His heart was in his throat.

Then, hoarse and trembling, he put out his
hands.

'Tell me it is not true!   Tell me it is not
true !'

'*What* is not true, Alan Carmichael ?'

'That that was he who died in the wood
yonder.'

'That was General Alasdair Carmichael.'

'My father ?'

'Your father.'

'But, you devil, you murdered him! I saw you do it! You knew it was he—and you killed him. You knew he would not try to kill you, and you waited: then, when he had fired, you took careful aim and killed him!'

'You reiterate, my friend. These are facts with which I am familiar.'

The cool, sneering tone stung Allan to madness. He advanced, menacingly.

'Murderer, you shall not escape!'

'A fitting sentiment, truly, from a man who wants to marry my daughter!'

'Marry your daughter! Marry the daughter of my father's murderer! I would sooner never see the face of woman again than do this thing.'

'Good. I am well content. And now, young man, you are of age: you have come into your patrimony, including your ruined keep on the island of Rona; and I will trouble you to go— to leave Kerival for good and all.'

Suddenly, without a word, Alan moved rapidly forward. With a light touch he laid his hand for a moment on the brow of the motionless man in the wheeled-chair.

'There, I lay upon you, Tristran de Kerival, the curse of the newly dead and of the living ! May the evil that you have done corrode your brain, and may your life silt away as sand, and may your soul know the second death.'

As he turned to leave the room he saw Kerbastiou standing in the doorway.

'Who are you to be standing there, Judik Kerbastiou ?' demanded the steward angrily.

'I am Rohan de Kerival. Ask this man here if I am not his son. Three days ago, the woman who was my mother died. She died a vagrant in the forest. But, nigh upon thirty years ago, she was legally married to the young Marquis Tristran de Kerival. I am their child.'

Alan glanced at the man he had cursed. A strange look had come into his ashy face.

'Her name ?' was all Tristran the Silent said.

'Annora Brizeux.'

'You have proofs ? '

'I have all the proofs.'

'You are only a peasant, I disown you. I know nothing of you or of the wanton that was your mother.'

Without a word Judik strode forward and struck him full in the face. At that moment the miraculous happened. The Marquise, who had not stood erect for years, rose to her full height.

She, too, crossed the room.

'Alan,' she cried, 'see: he has killed me as well as your father,' and with that she swayed, and fell dead, at the feet of the man who had trampled her soul in the dust and made of her blossoming life a drear and sterile wilderness.

BOOK SECOND

THE HERDSMAN

CHAPTER I

At the end of the third month after that disastrous day when Alan Carmichael knew that
his father had been slain, and before his unknow-
ing eyes, by Tristran de Kerival, a great terror
came upon him.

On that day itself he had left the Manor of
Kerival. With all that blood between him and
his enemy he could not stay a moment longer in
the house. To have done so would have been to
show himself callous indeed to the memory of his
father.

Nor could he see Ynys. He could not look
at her, innocent as she was. She was her father's
child, and her father had murdered his father.
Surely a union would be against nature: he
must fly while he had the strength.

When, however, he had gained the yew-close
he turned, hesitated, and then slowly walked
northward to where the long brown dunes lay
in a golden glow overagainst the pale blue of
the sea.   There, bewildered, wrought almost to
madness, he moved to and fro, unable to realise
all that had happened, and with bitter words
cursing the malign fate which had overtaken
him.

The afternoon waned, and he was still there,
uncertain as ever, still confused, baffled, mentally
blind.

Then suddenly he saw the figure of Yann the
Dumb, his friend and clansman, Ian Macdonald.
The old man had understood at once that, after
what had happened, Alan Carmichael would
never go back to Kerival.

'Why do you come to see me here, Ian?'
Alan had asked wearily.

When Ian began ' *Thiginn gu d'choimhead*
. . . I would come to see you, though your
home were a rock-cave,' the familiar sound of
the Gaelic did more than anything else to clear
his mind of the shadows which overlay it.

'Yes, Alan MacAlasdair,' Ian answered, in response to an eager question, 'whatever I know is yours now, since Lois nic Choinneach is dead, poor lady: though, sure, it is the best thing she could be having now, that death.'

As swiftly as possible Alan elicited all he could from the old man: all that there had not been time to hear from the Marquise. He learned what a distinguished soldier, what a fine man, what a true Gael, Alasdair Carmichael had been. When his wife had died he had been involved in some disastrous lawsuit, and his deep sorrow and absolute financial ruin came to him at one and the same moment. It was at this juncture, though there were other good reasons also, that Lois de Kerival had undertaken to adopt and bring up Silis's child. When her husband Tristran had given his consent, it was with the stipulation that Lois and Alasdair Carmichael should never meet, and that the child was not to learn his surname till he came into the small fortune due to him through his mother.

This and much else Alan learned from Ian. Out

of all the pain grew a feeling of bitter hatred for the cold, hard man who had wrought so much unhappiness; and, were it not for Ynys and Annaik he would, for the moment, have rejoiced that in Judik Kerbastiou Nemesis had appeared. At his first mention of the daughters, Ian had looked at him closely.

'Will you be for going back to that house, Alan MacAlasdair?' he asked, and in a tone so marked that even in his distress Alan noticed it.

'Do you wish me to go back, Ian?'

'God forbid. I hear the dust on the threshold rising at the thought.'

'We are both in an alien land, Ian.'

'*Och is diombuan gach cas air tìr gun eòlas*— Fleeting is the foot in a strange land,' said the islander, using a phrase familiar to Gaels away from the isles.

'But what can I do?'

'Sure you can go to your own place, Alan MacAlasdair. There you can think of what you will do. And before you go I must tell you that your father's brother Uilleam is dead, so that you have no near kin now except the son of the brother of your father, Donnacha Bàn as he is called—or was called, for I will be hearing a year or more ago that he, too, went under the wave. He would be your own age, and that close as a month or week, I am thinking.'

'Nevertheless, Ian, I cannot go without seeing my cousin Ynys once more.'

'You will never be for marrying the daughter of the man that murdered your father?' Ian spoke in horrified amaze, adding: 'Sure, if that were so, it would indeed mean that they may talk as they like of this southland as akin to Gaeldom, though that is not a thought that will bring honey to the hive of my brain—for no man of the isles would ever forget *there* that the blood of a father cries up to the stars themselves.'

'Have you no message for me, from . . . from . . . her ?'

'Ay,' answered the old islesman reluctantly, 'here it is. I did not give it to you before, for fear you should be weak.'

Without a word, Alan snatched the pencilled

note.   It had no beginning or signature, and
ran simply: 'My mother is dead, too.   After
all that has happened to-day I know we cannot
meet.   I know, too, that I love you with all
my heart and soul: that I have given you my
deathless devotion.   But, unless you say "Come,"
it is best that you go away at once, and that
we never see each other again.'

At that, Alan had torn off the half sheet,
and written a single word upon it.

It was: *Come.*

This he gave to Ian, telling him to go straightway with it, and hand the note to Ynys
in person. 'Also,' he added, 'fulfil unquestion-
ingly everything she may tell you to do or not
to do.'

An hour or more after Ian had gone, and
when a dark still gloaming had begun, he came
again, but this time with Ynys.

He and she walked together: behind them
came four horses, led by Ian.   When the lovers
met, they stood silent for some moments.   Then
Ynys, knowing what was in Alan's mind, asked
if she were come for life or death.

'I love you, dear,' was his answer: 'I cannot live without you. If you be in truth the daughter of the man who slew my father, why should his evil blood be our undoing also? God knows but that even thus may his punishment be begun. All his thoughts were upon you and Annaik.'

'Annaik is gone.'

'Gone! Annaik gone! Where has she gone?'

'I know nothing. She sent me a line to say that she would never sleep in Kerival again: that something had changed her whole life: that she would return three days hence for our mother's funeral: and that thereafter she and I would never meet.'

In a flash, Alan saw many things; but deepest of all he saw the working of doom. On the very day of his triumph, Tristran de Kerival had lost all, and found only that which made life more bitter than death. Stammeringly, now, Alan sought to say something about Annaik, that there was a secret, an unhappiness, a sorrow, which he must explain.

But at that Ynys had pointed to the dim grey-brown sea.

'There, Alan, let us bury it all there; everything, everything! Either you and I must find our forgetfulness there, or we must drown therein all this terrible past which has an inexplicable, a menacing present. Dear, I am ready. Shall it be life or death?'

'Life.'

That was all that was said. Alan leaned forward, and, tenderly kissing her, took her in his arms. Then he turned to Ian.

'Ian mac Iain, I call you to witness that I take Ynys de Kerival as my wife; that in this taking, all the blood-feud that lies betwixt us is become as nought; and that the past is past. Henceforth I am Alan Carmichael, and she here is Ynys Carmichael.'

At that, Ian had bowed his head. It was against the tradition of his people; but he loved Ynys as well as Alan, and secretly he was glad.

Thereafter, Alan and Ynys had mounted, and ridden slowly southward through the dusk;

while Ian followed on the third horse, with, in rein, its companion, on which were the apparel and other belongings which Ynys had hurriedly put together.

They were unmolested in their flight. Indeed, they met no one, till, at the end of the Forest of Kerival, they emerged near the junction with the high road at a place called Trois Chênes. Then a woman, a gypsy vagrant, insisted disaster would ensue if they went over her tracks that night without first doing something to avert evil. They must cross her hand with silver, she said.

Impatient as he was, Alan stopped, and allowed the gypsy to have her will.

She looked at the hand Ynys held out through the obscurity, and almost immediately dropped it.

'Beware of crossing the sea,' she said: 'I see your death floating on a green wave.'

Ynys shuddered, but said nothing. When Alan put out his hand the woman held it in hers for a few seconds, and then pondered it intently.

'Be quick, my good woman,' he urged, 'we are in a hurry.'

' It will be behind the shadow when we meet again,' was all her reply : enigmatical words, which yet in his ears had a sombre significance. But he was even more perturbed by the fact that, before she relinquished his hand, she stooped abruptly and kissed it.

As the fugitives rode onward slowly along the dusky high-road, Alan whispered to Ynys that he could not forget the gypsy : that in some strange way she haunted him : and even seemed to him to be linked to that disastrous day.

' That may well be,' Ynys had answered : ' for the woman was Annaik.'

Onward they rode till they came to Haut-Kerloek, the ancient village on the slope of the hill above the little town. There, at the ' Gloire de Kerival' they stopped for the night. Next morning they resumed their journey, and the same afternoon reached St. Blaise-sur-Loise, where they knew they would find the body of General Alasdair Carmichael.

And it was thus that, by the strange irony of fate, Alasdair Carmichael, who had never seen

his son, who in turn had unknowingly witnessed
his father's tragic death, was followed to the
grave-side by that dear child for whom he had
so often longed, and that by Alan's side was the
daughter of the man who had done so much to
ruin his life and had at the last slain him. At
the same hour, on the same day, Lois de Kerival
was laid to her rest, with none of her kith and
kin to lament her: for Tristran the Silent was
alone in his austere grief. Two others were
there, at whom the Curé looked askance: the
rude woodlander, Judik Kerbastiou, and another
forest estray, a gypsy woman with a shawl over
her head. The latter must have known the
Marquise's charity, for the good woman wept
quietly throughout the service of committal,
and, when she turned to go, the Curé heard
a sob in her throat.

It took but a brief while for Alan to settle
his father's few affairs. Among the papers, he
found one addressed to himself: a long letter
wherein was set forth not only all necessary
details concerning Alan's mother and father,
but also particulars about the small fortune that

was in keeping for him in Edinburgh, and the
lonely house on the lonely isle of Rona, among
the lonely Hebrides.

In St. Blaise Alan and Ynys went before the
civil authorities, and were registered as man and
wife. The next day they resumed their journey
towards that exile which they had in view.

Thereafter, slowly, and by devious ways, they
fared far north. At Edinburgh Alan had learned
all that was still unexplained. He found that
there would be enough money to enable Ynys and
himself to live quietly, particularly at so remote
a place as Rona. The castle or 'keep' there was
unoccupied, and had, indeed, long been un-
tenanted save by the widow woman Kirsten Macdonald, Ian's sister. In return for this home she
had kept the solitary place in order. All the
furniture that had been there, when Alasdair
Carmichael was last in Rona, remained. In
going thither, Alan and Ynys would be going
home.

The westward journey was a revelation to
them. Never had there been so beautiful a
May, they were told. They had lingered long

at the first place where they heard the sweet familiar sound of the Gaelic. Hand in hand, they wandered over the hillsides of which the very names had a poignant home-sweetness: and long hot hours they spent together on lochs of which Lois de Kerival had often spoken with deep longing in her voice.

As they neared the extreme of the mainland Alan's excitement deepened. He spoke hardly a word on the day the steamer left the Argyll coast behind, and headed for the dim isles of the sea, Coll and Tiree: and again on the following day Ynys saw how distraught he was, for, about noon, the coast-line of Uist loomed faintly blue upon the dark Atlantic horizon.

At Loch Boisdale, where they disembarked, and whence they had to sail the remainder of their journey in a fishing-schooner, which by good fortune was then there, and disengaged, Ian was for the first time recognised. All that evening, Alan and Ynys talked with the islesmen, Alan finding to his delight his Gaelic was so good that none for a moment suspected he had not lived in the isles all his life. That of Ynys, however, though fluent, had a foreign sound which puzzled the admiring fishermen.

It was an hour after sunrise when the *Blue Herring* sailed out of Loch Boisdale, and it was an hour before sunset when the anchor dropped in Borosay Haven.

On this night Alan perceived the first sign of aloofness among his fellow-Gaels. Hitherto every one had been cordial, and he and Ynys had rejoiced in the courtesy and genial friendliness which they had everywhere encountered.

But in Balnarec ('Baille'-na-Righ'), the little village wherein was focussed all that Borosay had to boast of in the way of civic life, he could not disguise from himself that again and again he was looked at askance.

Rightly or wrongly he took this to be resentment because of his having wed Ynys, the daughter of the man who had murdered Alasdair Carmichael. So possessed was he by this idea that he did not remember how little likely the islanders were to know aught concerning Ynys, or indeed anything beyond the fact that Alasdair MacAlasdair Rhona had died abroad.

The trouble became more than an imaginary one when, on the morrow, he tried to find a boat for the passage to Rona. But for the Frozen Hand, as the triple-peaked hill to the south of Balnaree was called, Rona would have been visible: nor was it, with a fair wind, more than an hour's sail distant.

Nevertheless, every one to whom he spoke showed a strange reluctance. At last, in despair, he asked an old man of his own surname why there was so much difficulty.

In the island way, Sheumas Carmichael replied that the people on Elleray, the island adjacent to Rona, were incensed.

'But incensed at what?'

'Well, at this and at that. But for one thing they are not having any dealings with the Carmichaels. They are all Macdonalds there, Macdonalds of Barra. There is a feud, I am thinking; though I know nothing of it, no, not I.'

'But, Seumas mac Eachainn, you know well yourself that there are almost no Carmichaels to have a feud with! There are you and your

brother, and there is your cousin over at Sgòrr-
Bhan on the other side of Borosay. Who else is
there?'

To this the man could say nothing. Distressed,
Alan sought Ian and bade him find out what he
could. He also, however, was puzzled and even
seriously perturbed. That some evil was at
work could not be doubted; and that it was
secret boded ill.

Ian was practically a stranger in Borosay
because of his long absence. But though this
for a time shut him off from his fellow-islanders,
and retarded his discovery of what strange
reason accounted for the apparently inexplicable
apathy shown by the fishermen of Balnaree—an
apathy, too, so much to their own disadvantage
—it enabled him, on the other hand, to make a
strong appeal to the clan-side of the islanders'
natures. After all, Ian mac Iain mhic Dhonuill
was one of them, and though he came there
with a man in the shadow (though this phrase
was not used in Ian's hearing) that was not his
fault.

Suddenly Ian remembered a fact that he should

have thought of at once. There was the old woman, his sister Silis. He would speak of her, and of their long separation, and of his desire to see her again before he died.

This made a difficult thing easy. Within an hour, a boat was ready to take the travellers to the Isle of the Caves—as Rona was called locally. Before the hour was gone, they, with the stores of food and other things they had been advised to take with them, were slipping seaward out of Borosay Haven.

The moment the headland was rounded the heights of Rona came into view. Great gaunt cliffs they are, precipices of black basalt: though on the south side they fall away in grassy declivities, which hang a greenness over the wandering wave for ever sobbing round that desolate shore. But it was not till the Sgòrr-Dhu, a conical black rock at the south-east end of the island, was reached that the stone keep, known as Caisteal Rhona, came in sight.

It stands at the landward extreme of a rocky ledge, on the margin of a green airidh. Westward is a small dark-blue sea-loch, no more than

a narrow haven. To the north-west rise sheer
the ocean-fronting precipitous cliffs : northward,
above the green pasture and a stretch of heather,
is a woodland-belt of some three or four hundred
pine-trees. It might well be called I-monair, as
Aodh the Islander sang of it : for it is ever
echoing with murmurous noises. If the waves
dash against it from the south or east, a loud
crying is upon the faces of the rocks ; if from
the north or north-east, there is a dull iteration,
and amid the pines a continual soughing sea-
voice. But when the wind blows from the south-
west, or the huge Atlantic billows surge out of
the west, Rona is a place filled with an indescribable tumult. Through the whole island goes the
myriad echo of a hollow booming, with an incessant sound as though waters were pouring
through vast hidden conduits in the heart of
every precipice, every rock, every boulder. This
is because of the arcades of which it consists,
for from the westward the island has been
honeycombed by the sea. No living man has
ever traversed all those mysterious winding sea-
galleries. Many have perished in the attempt.

In the olden days the Uisteans and Barrovians sought refuge there from the marauding Danes and other pirates out of Lochlin: and in the time when the last Scottish king took shelter in the west many of his island-followers found safety among these perilous arcades.

Some of them reach to an immense height. These are filled with a pale green gloom, which in fine weather, and at noon or towards sundown, becomes almost radiant. But most have only a dusky green obscurity, and some are at all times dark with a darkness that has seen neither sun, nor moon, nor star for unknown ages. Sometimes, there, a phosphorescent wave will spill a livid or a cold blue flame, and for a moment a vast gulf of dripping basalt be revealed; but day and night, night and day, from year to year, from age to age, that awful wave-clamant darkness prevails unbroken.

To the few who know some of the secrets of the Passages, it is possible, except when a gale blows from any quarter but the north, to thrid these dim arcades in a narrow boat, and so to pass from the Hebrid Seas to the outer Atlantic.

But to one unaware of the clues there might well be no return to the light of the open day: for in that maze of winding galleries and dim, sea-washed and for ever unlitten arcades, there is only a hopeless bewilderment. Once bewildered, there is no hope; and the lost adventurer will remain there idly drifting from barren corridor to corridor, till he perish of hunger and thirst, or, maddened by the strange and appalling gloom and the unbroken silence—for there the muffled voice of the sea is no more than a whisper—he leap into the green waters which for ever slide stealthily from ledge to ledge.

From Ian mac Iain Alan had heard of such an isle, though he had not known it to be Rona. Now, as he approached his wild remote home he thought of these death-haunted corridors, avenues of the grave as they are called in the 'Cumha Fhir-Mearanach Aonghas mhic Dhonuill —the Lament of mad Angus Macdonald.'

When, at last, the unwieldy brown coble sailed into the little haven, it was to create unwonted excitement among the few fishermen who put in there frequently for bait. A group of eight or

ten was upon the rocky ledge beyond Caisteal-
Rhona, among them the elderly woman who was
sister to Ian mac Iain.

At Alan's request, Ian went ashore in advance,
in a small punt. He was to wave his hand if all
were well, for Alan could not but feel appre-
hensive on account of the strange ill-will that
had shown itself at Borosay.

It was with relief that he saw the signal when,
after Ian had embraced his sister, and shaken
hands with all the fishermen, he had explained
that the son of Alasdair Carmichael was come
out of the south, and with a beautiful young
wife, too, and was henceforth to live at Caisteal-
Rhona.

All there uncovered, and waved their hats.
Then a shout of welcome went up, and Alan's
heart was glad, and that of Ynys.

But the moment he had set foot on land he
saw a startled look come into the eyes of the
fishermen, a look that deepened swiftly into one
of aversion, almost of fear.

One by one the men moved away, awkward
in their embarrassment. Not one came forward

with outstretched hand, nor said a word of welcome.

At first amazed, then indignant, Ian reproached them. They received his words in ashamed silence. Even when with a bitter tongue he taunted them, they answered nothing.

'Silis,' said Ian, turning in despair to his sister, 'what is the meaning of this folly?'

But even she was no longer the same. Her eyes were fixed upon Alan with a look of dread and indeed of horror. It was unmistakable, and Alan himself was conscious of it, with a strange sinking of the heart.

'Speak, woman,' he demanded. 'What is the meaning of this thing? Why do you and these men look at me askance?'

'God forbid,' answered Silis Macdonald with white lips; 'God forbid that we look at the son of Alasdair Carmichael askance. But——'

'But what?'

With that the woman put her apron over her head and moved away, muttering strange words.

'Ian, what is this mystery?'

It was Ynys who spoke now, for on Alan's face was a shadow, and in his eyes a deep gloom. She too was white, and had fear in her eyes.

'How am I for knowing, Ynys-nighean-Lhois? It is all a darkness to me also. But I will find out.'

That, however, was easier for Ian to say than to do. Meanwhile, the brown coble tacked back to Borosay, and the fishermen sailed away to the Barra coasts, and Alan and Ynys were left solitary in their wild and remote home.

But in that very solitude they found healing. From what Giorsal hinted, they came to believe that the fishermen had experienced one of those strange dream-waves which, in remote isles, occur at times, when whole communities will be wrought by the self-same fantasy. When day by day went past, and no one came nigh them, at first they were puzzled and even resentful, but this passed, and soon they were glad to be alone. Only Ian knew that there was another cause for the inexplicable aversion that had been shown. But he was silent, and he

kept a patient watch for the hour that the future
held in its dim shroud. As for Silis, she was
dumb : but no more looked at Alan askance.

And so the weeks went. Occasionally a fishing
smack came with the provisions, for the weekly
despatch of which Alan had arranged at Loch
Boisdale, and sometimes the Barra men put in
at the haven, though they would never stay
long, and always avoided Alan as much as was
possible.

In that time Alan and Ynys came to know
and love their strangely beautiful island home.
Hours and hours at a time they spent exploring
the dim, green, winding sea-galleries, till at last
they knew the main corridors thoroughly. They
even ventured into some of the narrow snake-
like passages, but never for long, because of the
awe and dread these held, silent estuaries of
the grave.

There, too, they forgot all the sorrow that
had been theirs, forgot the shadow of death
which lay between them. They buried all in
the deep sea of love that was about the rock
of their passion. For, as of another Alan and

another woman, the *mirdhei* was upon them : the dream-spell of love.

Day by day, with them as with that Alan and Sorcha of whom they had often heard, their joy had grown, like a flower moving ever to the sun ; and as it grew the roots deepened, and the tendrils met and intertwined round the two hearts, till at last they were drawn together and became one, as two moving rays of light will converge into one beam, or the song of two singers blend and become as the song of one.

As the weeks passed, the wonder of the dream became at times a brooding passion, at times almost an ecstasy. Ossian and the poets of old speak of a strange frenzy that came upon the brave : and, sure, there is a *mircath* of another kind now and again in the world, in the green, remote places at least. Aodh the islander, and Ian-Bàn of the hills, and other dreamer-poets know of it—the *mirdhei*, the passion that is deeper than passion, the dream that is beyond the dream. This, that was once the fair doom of another Alan and Sorcha, of whom Ian had often told him with hushed voice and dreaming eyes, was now upon himself and Ynys.

They were Love to each other. In each the other saw the beauty of the world. Hand in hand they wandered among the wind-haunted pines, or along the thyme and grass of the summits of the precipices: or they sailed for hours upon the summer seas, blue lawns of moving azure, glorious with the sun-dazzle and lovely with purple cloud-shadows and amethystine straits of floating weed: or, by noontide, or at the full of the moon, they penetrated far into the dim green arcades, and were as shadows in a strange and fantastic but ineffably sweet and beautiful dream.

Day was lovely and desirable to each, for day dreamed to night: and night was sweet as life because it held the new day against its dark beating heart. Week after week passed, and to Ynys as to Alan it was as the going of the grey-owl's wing, swift and silent.

*   *   *   *   *

*   *   *   *   *

Then it was that, on a day of the days, Alan was suddenly stricken with a new and startling dread.

CHAPTER II

In the hour that this terror came upon him, Alan was alone upon the high slopes of Rona, where the grass fails and the moor purples at an elevation of close on a thousand feet above the sea.

The day had been cloudless since sunrise. The immeasurable range of ocean expanded like the single petal of an azure flower: all of one unbroken blue save for the shadows of the scattered isles and for the fugitive amethyst where floating weed suspended. An immense number of birds congregated from every quarter. Guillemots and skuas and puffins, cormorants and northern-divers, everywhere darted, swam, or slept upon the listless sea, whose deep suspiration no more than lifted a league-long calm here and there, to lapse insensibly even as it rose. Through the not less silent quietudes of air the sea-gulls swept with curving flight, and the narrow-winged terns made a constant shimmer. At remote altitudes the gannet motionlessly drifted. Ocean-ward the great widths of calm were rent now and again by the shoulders of the porpoises which followed the herring-trail, their huge black revolving bodies looming large above the silent wave. Not a boat was visible anywhere: not even upon the most distant horizons did a brown sail fleck itself duskily against the skyward wall of steely blue.

In the great stillness which prevailed, the noise of the surf beating around the promontory of Aonaig was audible as a whisper: though even in that windless hour the indescribable rumour of the sea moving through the arcades of the island filled the hollow of the air overhead. Ever since the early morning, Alan had moved under a strange gloom. Out of that golden glory of midsummer a breath of joyous life should have reached his heart, but it was not so.

For sure, there is sometimes in the quiet beauty
of summer an air of menace, a breath, a suspicion, a dream-premonition, of suspended force,
a force antagonistic and terrible. All who have
lived in these lonely isles know the peculiar intensity of this summer melancholy. No clamour
of tempestuous wind, no prolonged sojourn of
untimely rains, no long baffling of mists in all
the drear inclemencies of that remote region, can
produce the same ominous and even paralys-
ing gloom which sometimes can be born of ineffable peace and beauty. Is it that in the
human soul there is mysterious kinship with the
outer soul which we call Nature: and that in
these few supreme hours which come at the full
of the year, we are sometimes suddenly aware of
the tremendous forces beneath and behind us,
momently quiescent?

Standing with Ynys upon a grassy headland,
Alan had looked long at the dream-blue perspectives to the southward, seeing there at first no
more than innumerable hidden pathways of the
sun, with blue-green and silver radiance immeasurable, and the very breath and wonder and

mystery of ocean life suspended as in a dream.
In the hearts of each, deep happiness brooded.
Perhaps it was out of these depths that rose the
dark flower of this sudden apprehension that
came upon him. It was no fear for Ynys,
nor for himself, not for the general weal:
but a profound disquietude, a sense of inevitable
ill. Ynys felt the tightening of his hand, and
saw the sudden change in his face. It was often
so with him. The sun-dazzle, at which he would
look with endless delight, finding in it a tangible
embodiment of the fugitive rhythms of cosmic
music which floated everywhere, would sometimes
be a dazzle also in his brain. In a moment a
strange bewilderment would render unstable
those perilous sands of the human brain which
are for ever laved by the strange waters of the
unseen life. When this mood or fantasy, or un-
calculable accident occurred, he was often wrought
either by vivid dreams, or creative work, or else
would lapse into a melancholy from which not
even the calling love of Ynys would arouse him.

When she saw in his face and in his eyes
this sudden bewildered look, and knew that in

M

some mysterious way the madness of the beauty
of the sea had enthralled him, she took his hand
and moved with him inland.   In a brief while
the poignant fragrance from the trodden thyme
and short hill-grass, warmed by the sun, rose as
an intoxication.   For that hour the gloom went.
But when, later, he wandered away from Caisteal-
Rhona, once more the sense of foreboding was
heavy upon him.   Determined to shake it off,
he wandered high among the upland solitudes.
There a cool air for ever moved even in the
noons of August: and there, indeed, at last,
there came upon him a deep peace.   With joy,
his mind dwelt over and over again upon all
that Ynys had been and was to him; upon the
depth and passion of their love; upon the mystery
and wonder of that coming life which was theirs
and yet was not of them, itself already no more
than an unrisen wave or an unbloomed flower,
but yet as inevitable as they, and dowered with
the light which is beyond where mortal shadows
end.   Strange, this passion of love for what
is not: strange this deep longing of the woman
—the longing of the womb, the longing of the

heart, the longing of the brain, the longing of the soul—for the perpetuation of the life she shares in common with one whom she loves : strange this longing of the man, a longing deep-based in his nature as the love of life or the fear of death, for the gaining, from the woman whom he loves, this personal hostage against oblivion. For, indeed, something of this so commonplace, and yet so divine and mysterious tide of birth, which is for ever at the flow upon this green world, is due to an instinctive fear of cessation. The perpetuation of life is the unconscious protest of humanity against the destiny of mortality. Thoughts such as these were often with Alan now : often, too, with Ynys, in whom indeed all the latent mysticism which had ever been a bond between them had latterly been continually evoked. Possibly it was the mere shadow of his great love; possibly it was some fear of the dark way wherein the sunrise of each new birth is involved ; possibly it was no more than the melancholy of the isles, that so wrought him on this perfect day. Whatsoever the reason, a deeper despondency prevailed as noon waned into afternoon,

An incident, deeply significant to him, in that
mood, at that time, happened then. A few
hundred yards away from where he stood, half
hidden in a little glen where a fall of water
made a continual spray among the shadows of
the rowan and birch, was the bothie of a woman,
the wife of Neil MacNeill, a fisherman of Aonaig.
She was there, he knew, for the summer pastur-
ing: and, even as he recollected this, he heard the
sound of her voice as she sang somewhere down
by the burn-side. Moving slowly towards the
corrie, he stopped at a mountain ash which over-
hung a deep pool. Looking down he saw the
woman, Morag MacNeill, washing and peeling
potatoes in the clear brown water. And as she
washed and peeled, she sang an old-time shealing
hymn of the Virgin-Shepherdess, of Michael the
White, and of Columan the Dove. It was a
song that, far away in Brittany, he had heard
Lois, the mother of Ynys, sing in one of those
rare hours when her youth came back to her with
something of youth's passionate intensity. He
listened now to every word of the doubly familiar
Gaelic, and when Morag finished, the tears were

in his eyes, and he stood for a while as one
entranced :—[1]

> ' *A Mhicheil mhin ! nan steud geala,*
> *A choisin cios air Dragon fala,*
> *Air ghaol Dia' us Mhic Muire,*
> *Sgaoil do sgiath oirnn dian sinn uile,*
> *Sgaoil do sgiath oirnn dian sinn uile.*
>
> *A Mhoire ghradhach ! Mathair Uain-ghil,*
> *Cohhair oirnne, Oigh na h-uaisle ;*
> *A rioghainn uai'reach ! a bhauchaille nan treud !*
> *Cum ar cuallach cuartaich sinn le cheil,*
> *Cum ar cuallach cuartaich sinn le cheil.*
>
> *A Chalum-Chille ! chairdeil, chaoimh,*
> *An ainm Athar, Mic, 'us Spioraid Naoimh,*
> *Trid na Trithinn ! trid na Triath !*
> *Comraig sinne, gleidh ar trial,*
> *Comraig sinne, gleidh ar trial.*
>
> *Athair ! A Mhic ! A Spioraid Naoimh !*
> *Bi'eadh an Tri-Aon leinn, a la 's a dh-oidhche !*
> *'S air chul nan tonn, no air thaobh nam beann,*
> *Bi'dh ar Mathair leinn, 's bith A lamh fo'r ceann,*
> *Bi'dh ar Màthair leinn, 's bith A lamh fo'r ceann.'*

---

[1] This hymn was taken down in the Gaelic and translated by
Mr. Alexander Carmichael of South Uist.

'Thou gentle Michael of the white steed,
Who subdued the Dragon of blood,
For love of God and the Son of Mary,
Spread over us thy wing, shield us all !
Spread over us thy wing, shield us all !

Mary Beloved ! Mother of the White Lamb,
Protect us, Thou Virgin of nobleness,
Queen of beauty ! Shepherdess of the flocks !
Keep our cattle, surround us together,
Keep our cattle, surround us together.

Thou Columba, the friendly, the kind,
In name of the Father, the Son, and the Spirit
    Holy,
Through the Three-in-One, through the Three,
Encompass us, guard our procession,
Encompass us, guard our procession.

Thou Father ! thou Son ! thou Spirit Holy !
Be the Three-One with us day and night,
And on the crested wave, or on the mountain side,
Our Mother is there, and Her arm is under our
    head,
Our Mother is there, and Her arm is under our
    head.'

After she had ceased, Alan found himself repeating whisperingly, and again and again,

'*Bi'eadh an Tri-Aon leinn, a la 's a dh-oidhche !*
'*S air chul nan tonn, no air thaobh nam beann.*'

Suddenly the woman glanced upward, perhaps because of the shadow that moved against the green bracken below. With a startled gesture, she sprang to her feet. Alan looked at her kindly, saying with a smile, 'Sure, Morag nic Tormaid, it is not fear you need be having of one who is your friend.' Then, seeing that the woman stared at him with intent gaze, wherein was terror as well as surprise, he spoke to her again.

'Sure, Morag, I am no stranger, that you should be looking at me with those foreign eyes.' He laughed as he spoke, and made as though he were about to descend to the burn-side. Unmistakably, however, the woman did not desire his company. He saw that, with the pain and bewilderment which had come upon him whenever the like happened, as so often it had happened since he had come to Rona.

'Tell me, Bean Neil MacNeill, what is the meaning of this strangeness that is upon you? Why do you not speak? Why do you turn away your head?'

Suddenly the woman flashed her black eyes upon him.

'Have you ever heard of *am Buchaille Bàn*— *am Buchaille Buidhe?*'

He looked at her in amaze. *Am Buchaille Bàn!* . . . The fair-haired Herdsman, the yellow-haired Herdsman! What could she mean? In days gone by, he knew, the islanders had, in the evil time after Culloden, so named the fugitive Prince who had sought shelter in the Hebrides : and in some of the runes of an older day still the Saviour of the World was sometimes so called, just as Mary was called *Bhuachaille nan treud*, Shepherdess of the Flocks. But, as Alan knew well, no allusion to either of these was intended.

'Who is the Herdsman of whom you speak, Morag?'

'Is it no knowledge you have of him at all Alan MacAlasdair?'

'None. I know nothing of the man, nothing of what is in your mind. Who is the Herdsman?'

'You will not be putting evil upon me because that you saw me here by the pool before I saw you?'

'Why should I, woman? Why do you think

that I have the power of the evil eye? Sure, I have done no harm to you or yours, and wish none. But if it is for peace to you to know it, it is no evil I wish you, but only good. The Blessing of Himself be upon you and yours and upon your house.'

The woman looked relieved, but still cast her furtive gaze upon Alan, who no longer attempted to join her.

'I cannot be speaking the thing that is in my mind, Alan MacAlasdair. It is not for me to be saying that thing. But if you have no knowledge of the Herdsman, sure it is only another wonder of the wonders, and God has the sun on that shadow, to the Stones be it said.'

'But tell me, Morag, who is the Herdsman of whom you speak?'

For a minute or more the woman stood regarding him intently. Then slowly, and as with difficulty, she spoke—

'Why have you appeared to the people upon the isle, sometimes by moonlight, sometimes by day or in the dusk? and have foretold upon one and all who dwell here black gloom and the red flame of sorrow? Why have you, who are an outcast because of what lies between you and another, pretended to be an emissary of the Son—ay, for sure, even, God forgive you, to be the Son Himself?'

Alan stared at the woman in blank amaze. For a time he could utter no word. Had some extraordinary delusion spread among the islanders, and was there in the insane accusation of this woman the secret of that inexplicable aversion which had so troubled him?

'This is all an empty darkness to me, Morag. Speak more plainly, woman. What is all this madness that you say? When have I uttered aught of having any mission, or of being other than I am? When have I foretold evil upon you or yours, or upon the isles beyond? What man has ever dared to say that Alan MacAlasdair of Rona is an outcast, and what sin is it that lies between me and another of which you know?'

It was impossible for Morag MacNeill to doubt the sincerity of the man who spoke to her. She crossed herself, and muttered the words of a *sian* for the protection of the soul against the demon powers. Still, even while she believed in Alan's sincerity, she could not reconcile it with that terrible and strange mystery with which rumour had filled her ears. So, having nothing to say in reply to his eager questions, she cast down her eyes and kept silence.

'Speak, Morag, for heaven's sake! Speak if you are a true woman, you that see a man in sore pain, in pain too for that of which he knows nothing, and of the ill of which he is guiltless!'

But, keeping her face averted, the woman muttered simply: 'I have no more to say.' With that she turned and moved slowly along the pathway which led from the pool to her hillside bothie.

With a sigh, Alan turned and moved across the moor. What wonder, he thought, that deep gloom had been upon him that day? Here, in the woman's mysterious words, was the shadow of that shadow.

Slowly, brooding deep over what he had heard, he traversed the Mona-nan-Con, as the hill-tract there was called, till he came to the rocky wilderness known as the Slope of the Caverns.

There for a time he leaned against a high boulder, idly watching a few sheep nibbling the short grass which grew about the apertures of some of the many caves which disclosed themselves in all directions. Below and beyond, he saw the illimitable calm beauty of the scene: southward, with no break anywhere; eastward, a sun-blaze void; south-westward, the faint, blue film of the coasts of Ulster; westward, the same immeasurable windless expanse. From where he stood he could just hear the murmur of the surge whispering all round the isle; the surge that even on days of profoundest calm makes a murmurous rumour among the rocks and shingle of the island shores. Not upon the moor side, but in the blank hollows of the caves around him, he heard, as in gigantic shells, the moving of a strange and solemn rhythm: wave-haunted shells indeed, for the echo that was bruited from one to the other came from beneath, from out of those labyrinthine corridors and dim shadowy arcades, wherethrough the intense green glooms the Atlantic waters lose themselves in a vain wandering.

For long he leaned there, revolving in his mind the mystery of Morag MacNeill's words. Then, abruptly, the stillness was broken by the sound of a dislodged stone. So little did he expect the foot of a fellow, that he did not turn at what he thought to be the slip of a sheep. But when upon the slope of the grass, just beyond where he stood, a dusky blue shadow wavered fantastically, he swung round with a sudden instinct of dread.

And this was the dread which, at the end of the third month after he and Ynys had come to Rona, was upon Alan Carmichael.

For, there, standing quietly by another boulder, at the mouth of another cave, stood a man who was in all appearances identical with himself. Looking at this apparition, he beheld one of the same height as himself, with hair of the same hue, with eyes the same, and features the same, with the same carriage, the same smile, even the same expression. No, it was there, and there alone, that a difference was.

Sick at heart, Alan wondered if he looked upon his own wraith. Familiar as he was with the legends of his people, it would be no strange thing to him that there, upon the hillside, should appear the phantasm of himself. Had not old Ian MacIan—and that, too, though far away in a strange land—seen the death of Lois Macdonald moving upward from her feet to her knees, from her knees to her waist, from her waist to her neck and, just before the end, how the shroud darkened along the face until it hid the eyes? Had he not often heard from her, from Ian, of the second self which so often appears beside the living when already the shadow of doom is upon him whose hours are numbered? Was this, then, the reason of what had been his inexplicable gloom? Was he. indeed at the extreme of life; was his soul amid shallows, already a rock upon a blank inhospitable shore? If not, who or what was this second self which leaned there negligently, looking at him with scornfully smiling lips, but with intent unsmiling eyes?

Then, slowly, there came into his mind this

thought: how could a phantom, that was itself intangible, throw a shadow upon the grass, as though it were a living corporeal being? Sure, a shadow there was indeed. It lay between the apparition and himself. A story heard in boyhood came back to him; instinctively, he stooped, and, lifting a stone, flung it midway into the shadow.

'Go back into the darkness,' he cried, 'if out of the darkness you came; but, if you be a living thing, put out your hands!'

The shadow remained motionless; though when Alan looked again at his second self he saw that the scorn which had been upon the lips was now in the eyes also. Ay, for sure, that was scornful laughter which lay in those cold wells of light. No phantom that; a man he, even as Alan himself. His heart pulsed like that of a trapped bird, but even in the speaking, his courage came back to him.

'Who are you?' he asked in a low voice that was strange even in his own ears.

'Am Buchaille,' replied the man in a voice as low and strange: 'I am the Herdsman.'

A new tide of fear surged in upon Alan.
That voice, was it not his own; that tone, was
it not familiar in his ears? When the man
spoke, he heard himself speak; sure, if he were
am Buchaille Bàn, Alan, too, was the Herdsman
—though what fantastic destiny might be his
was all unknown to him.

'Come near,' said the man, and now the
mocking light in his eyes was lambent as cloud-
fire : ' come near, O Buchaille Bàn ! '

With a swift movement, Alan leapt forward,
but as he leaped his foot caught in a spray of
heather, and he stumbled and nigh fell. When
he recovered himself, he looked in vain for the
man who had called him. There was not a sign,
not a trace of any living being. For the first few
moments he believed it had all been a delusion.
Mortal being did not appear and vanish in that
ghostly way. Still, surely he could not have
mistaken the blank of that place for a speaking
voice, nor out of nothingness have fashioned the
living phantom of himself ? Or could he ? With
that, he strode forward and peered into the wide
arch of the cavern by which the man had stood.

He could not see far into it, but so far as it was
possible to see, he discerned neither man nor
shadow of man, nor anything that stirred; no,
not even the dust of a bearnan-bride, that grew
on a patch of grass a yard or two within the darkness, had lost one of its aerial pinions.   He drew
back, dismayed.   Then, suddenly, his heart leapt
again, for, beyond all question, all possible doubt,
there, in the bent thyme just where the man had
stood, was the imprint of his feet.   Even now
the green sprays were moving forward.

CHAPTER III

MYSTERY

An hour passed, and Alan Carmichael still stood by the entrance to the cave. So immovable was he that a ewe listlessly wandering there in search of cooler grass lay down after a while, drowsily regarding him with her amber-coloured eyes. All his thought was intent upon the mystery of what he had seen. No delusion this, he was sure. That was a man whom he had seen. It might well have been some one whom he did not know, though that were unlikely, of course, for on so small an island, inhabited by less than a score of crofters, it was scarcely possible for one to live there for many weeks and not know the name and face of every soul upon the isle. Still, a stranger might have come. Only, if this were so, why should he call himself the Herdsman?

There was but one herdsman on Rona, and he
Angus MacCormic, who lived at Einaval on the
north side. In these outer isles the shepherd and
the herdsman are appointed by the community,
and no man is allowed to be one or the other
at will, any more than to be *maor* or *constabal*.
Then, too, if this man were indeed herdsman,
where was his *imir ionailt*, his browsing tract?
Looking round him Alan could perceive nowhere
any fitting pasture. Surely no herdsman would
be content with such an *imir a bhuchaille*—rig
of the herdsman—as that rocky wilderness, where
the soft green grass grew in patches under this
or that boulder, on the sun-side of this or that
mountain-ash. Again, he had given no name,
but called himself simply *Am Buchaille*. This
was how the woman Morag had spoken: did
she indeed mean this very man, and, if so, what
import lay in her words? But far beyond all
other bewilderment for him was that strange,
that indeed terrifying likeness to himself: a likeness so absolute, so convincing, that he knew he
might himself easily have been deceived had he
beheld the apparition in any place where it was

possible that a reflection could have misled
him.

Brooding thus, eye and ear were both intent
for the faintest sight or sound. But, from the
interior of the cavern, not a breath came. Once,
from among the jagged rocks high on the west
slope of Ben Einaval, he fancied he heard an
unwonted sound: that of human laughter, but
laughter so wild, so remote, so unmirthful, that
fear was in his heart. It could not be other
than imagination, he said to himself: for in
that lonely place there was none to wander idly
at that season, and none who, wandering, would
laugh there, solitary.

It was with an effort that Alan at last determined to probe the mystery. Stooping, he
moved cautiously into the cavern, and groped
his way along a narrow ledge which led, as he
thought, into another larger cave. But this
proved to be one of the innumerable hollow
corridors which intersect the honeycombed slopes
of the Isle of Caves. To wander far in these
lightless passages would be to court inevitable
death. Long ago the piper whom the Prionnsa-

Bàn, the Fair Prince, loved to hear in his exile,
he that was called Rory M'Vurich, penetrated
one of the larger hollows to seek there for a child
that had idly wandered into the dark. Some
of the clansmen, with the father and mother of
the little one, waited at the entrance to the cave.
For a time there was silence: then, as agreed
upon, the sound of the pipes was heard, to which
a man named Lachlan M'Lachlan replied from
the outer air. The skirl of the pipes within
grew fainter and fainter. Louder and louder
Lachlan played upon his *chantar*; shriller and
shriller grew the wild cry of the *feadan*; but for
all that, fainter and fainter waned the sound of
the pipes of Rory M'Vurich. Generations have
come and gone upon the isle, and still no man
has heard the returning air which Rory was to
play. He may have found the little child, but
he never found his backward path, and in the
gloom of that honeycombed hill he and the child
and the music of the pipes lapsed into the same
stillness. Remembering this legend, familiar to
him since his boyhood, Alan did not dare to
venture farther. At any moment, too, he knew

he might fall into one of the innumerable crevices
which opened into the sea-corridors hundreds of
feet below. Ancient rumour had it that there
were mysterious passages from the upper heights
of Ben Einaval, which led into the intricate
heart mazes of these perilous arcades. But
for a time he lay still, straining every sense.
Convinced at last that the man whom he sought
had evaded all possible quest, he turned to re-
gain the light. Brief way as he had gone, this
was no easy thing to do. For a few moments,
indeed, Alan lost his self-possession when he
found a uniform dusk about him, and could
scarce discern which of the several branching
narrow corridors was that by which he had
come. But following the greener light he
reached the cave, and soon, with a sigh of
relief, was upon the sun-sweet warm earth
again.

How more than ever beautiful the world
seemed to him : how sweet upon the eyes were
cliff and precipice, the wide stretch of ocean,
the flying birds, the sheep grazing on the scanty
pastures, and, above all, the homely blue smoke

curling faintly upward from the fisher crofts on the headland east of Aonaig.

Purposely he retraced his steps by the way of the glen. He would see the woman Morag MacNeill again, and insist on some more explicit word; but, when he reached the burnside once more, the woman was not there. Possibly she had seen him coming, and guessed his purpose: half he surmised this, for the peats in the hearth were brightly aglow, and on the hob beside them the boiling water hissed in a great iron pot, wherein were potatoes. In vain he sought, in vain called. Impatient at last he walked around the bothie and into the little byre beyond. The place seemed deserted. The matter, small as it was, added to his profound disquietude. Resolved to sift the mystery, he began to walk swiftly down the slope. By the old shealing of Cnoc-na-Monie, now forsaken, his heart leaped at sight of Ynys coming to meet him. At first he thought he would say nothing of what had happened. But with Ynys his was ever an impossible silence, for she knew every change in his mind as a seaman knows the

look of the sky and sea. Moreover, she had herself been all day oppressed by something of the
same inexplicable apprehension.

When they met she put her hands on his
shoulders, and looked at him lovingly with questioning eyes. Ah, he found rest and hope in
those deep pools of quiet light, whence the dreaming love rose comfortingly to meet his own yearning gaze.

'What is it, Alan mo-ghray, what is the
trouble that is upon you?'

'It is a trouble, Ynys, but one of which I can
speak little, for it is little I know.'

'Have you heard or seen aught that gives you
fear?'

'I have seen a man here upon Rona whom I
have not seen or met before, and it is one whose
face is known to me, and whose voice too, and
one whom I would not meet again.'

'Did he give you no name, Alan?'

'None.'

'Whence did he come? Whither did he go?'

'He came out of the shadow, and into the
shadow he went.'

Ynys looked steadfast at her husband, her
wistful gaze searching deep into his unquiet eyes,
and thence from feature to feature of the face,
which had become strangely worn, for all the joy
that lay between them.

But she said no more upon what he had told
her.

'I, too, Alan mo rùn, have heard a strange
thing to-day. You know old Marsail Macrae?
She is ill now with a slow fever, and she thinks
that the shadow which she saw lying upon her
hearth last Sabbath, when nothing was there
to cause any shadow, was her own death, come
for her, and now waiting there. I spoke to the
old woman comfortingly, but she would not have
peace, and her eyes looked at me strangely.

'"What is it, Marsail?" I asked at last. To
which she replied mysteriously—

'"Ay, ay, for sure, it was I who saw you
first."

'"Saw me first, Marsail?"

'"Ay, you and Alan MacAlasdair."

'"When and where was this sight upon you
that you speak of?"

' " It was one month before you and he came
to Rona."

' This startled me, and I asked her to tell
me her meaning. At first, I could make little
of what was said, for she muttered low, and
moved her head idly this way and that,
moaning in her pain. But on my taking her
hand, she looked at me again; and then, apparently without an effort, told me this thing :

' " On the seventh day of the month before you
came, and by the same token it was on the
seventh day of the month following that you
and Alan MacAlasdair came to Caisteal-Rhona,
I was upon the shore at Aonaig, listening to
the crying of the wind against the great precipice of Biolacreag. With me were Roderick
Macrae and Neil MacNeill, Morag MacNeill
and her sister Elsa, and we were singing the
hymn for those who were out on the wild sea
that was roaring white against the cliffs of
Berneray, for some of our people were there,
and we feared for them. Sometimes one sang
and sometimes another. And, sure, it is remem-

bering I am, how when I had called out with
my old wailing voice—

> ' *Biodh an Tri-aon leinn, a lu 's a dh-oidche;*
> *'S air chul nan tonn, no air thaobh nam beann.*—

> ' Be the Three-in-One with us day and night;
> On the crested wave, when waves run high.'—

I had just sung this, and we were all listening
to the sound of it caught by the wind and
whirled up against the black face of Biolacreag,
when suddenly I saw a boat come sailing quite
into the haven. I called out to those about
me, but they looked at me with white faces,
for no boat was there, and it was a rough,
wild sea it was in that haven.

' " And in that boat I saw three people sitting,
and one was you, Ynys nighean Lhois, and one
was Alan MacAlasdair, and one was a man
who had his face in shadow, and his eyes
looked into the shadow at his feet. I knew
not who you were, nor whence you came, nor
whether it was for Rona you were, nor anything at all; but I saw you clear, and I told
those about me what I saw. And Seumas

MacNeill, him that is dead now, and brother to
Neil here at Aonaig, he said to me: 'Who was
that whom you saw walking in the dusk the
night before last?' 'Alasdair MacAlasdair
Carmichael,' answered one at that. Seumas
muttered, looking at those about him, 'Mark
what I say, for it is a true thing; that Alasdair
Carmichael of Rona is dead now, because Marsail
here saw him walking in the dusk when he was
not upon the island; and now you, Neil, and
you, Roderick, and all of you will be for thinking with me that the man and the woman in
the boat whom Marsail sees now will be the son
and the daughter of him who has changed.'

' "Well, well, it is a true thing that we each
of us thought that thought, but when the days
went and nothing more came of·it, the memory
of the seeing went too. Then there came the
day when the coble of Aulay MacAulay came
out of Borosay into Caisteal-Rhona haven. Glad
we were to see the face of Ian mac Iain again,
and to hear the sob of joy coming out of the
heart of Silis his sister: but when you and
Alan MacAlasdair came on shore, it was my

voice that then went from mouth to mouth,
for I whispered to Morag MacNeill who was
next me, that you were the twain that I had
seen in the boat."

'Well, Alan,' Ynys added, with a grave
smile, 'I spoke gently to old Marsail, and told
her that after all there was no evil in that
seeing, and that for sure it was nothing at all,
at all, to see two people in a boat, and nothing
coming of that, save happiness for those two,
and glad content to be here, with hope like a
white swallow nesting for aye under the eaves
of our house.

'Marsail looked at me with big eyes.

'"It is no white swallow that builds there,
Ynys Bean Alan," she said.

'But when I asked her what she meant by that,
she would say no more. No asking of mine
would bring the word to her lips; only she
shook her head and averted her gaze from my
face. Then, seeing that it was useless, I said
to her—

'"Marsail, tell me this: was that sight of

yours the sole thing that made the people here
on Rona look askance at Alan MacAlasdair?"

'For a time she stared at me, with the dim
unrecognising eyes of those who are ill and in
the shadow of death; then, suddenly, they
brightened, and she spoke—

'"It is not all."

'"Then what more is there, Marsail Macrae?"

'"That is not for the saying. I have no more
to say. Let you, or your man, go elsewhere:
that which is to be, will be. To each his own
end."

'"Then tell me this at least," I asked, "is there
peril for Alan or for me in this island?"

'But from that moment Marsail would say no
more, and indeed I saw that a swoon was upon
the old woman, and that she heard not or saw
not.'

After this, Ynys and Alan walked slowly
home together, hand in hand, both silent and
revolving in their mind, as in a dim dusk,
that mystery which, vague and unreal at first,
had now become a living presence, and haunted
them by day and night.

CHAPTER IV

' In the shadow of pain, one may hear the footsteps of joy.' So runs a proverb of old.

It was a true saying for Alan and Ynys. That night they lay down in pain, their hearts heavy with the weight of some burden which they felt and did not know. On the morrow they woke to the rapture of a new day, a day of absolute beauty, when the stars grew pale in the cloudless blue sky before the uprising of the sun, while the last vapour lifted a white wing from the sea, and a dim spiral mist carried skyward the memory of inland dews. The whole wide wilderness of ocean was of living azure aflame with gold and silver. Around the promontories of the isles, the brown-sailed fish-boats of Barra and Berneray, of Borosay and Seila, moved blithely hither and thither. Everywhere the rhythm of life pulsed swift and

strong. The first sound which had awakened the
sleepers was of a loud singing of fishermen who
were putting out from Aonaig. The coming of
a great shoal of mackerel had been signalled, and
every man and woman of the near isles was alert
for the take. The first sign had been the swift
congregation of birds, particularly the gannets
and skuas. And as the men pulled at the oars,
or hoisted the brown sails, they sang a snatch of
an old-world tune, wont to be chanted at the first
coming of the birds when spring-tide is on the
flow again :—

> *' Bui' cheas dha 'n Ti thaine na Gugachan*
> *Thaine 's na h-Eoin-Mhora cuideriu,*
> *Cailin dugh ciaru bo 's a chro!*
> *Bo dhonn! bo dhonn! bo dhonn bheadarrach!*
> *Bo dhonn a ruin a bhlitheadh am baine dhuit*
> *Ho ro! mo gheallag! ni gu rodagach!*
> *Cailin dugh ciaru bo 's a chro,—*
> *Na h-eoin air tighinn! cluinneam an ceol!'*

> ' Thanks to the Being, the Gannets have come,
> Yes ! and the Great Auks along with them.
> Dark-haired girl !—a cow in the fold !
> Brown cow ! brown cow ! brown cow, beloved ho !
> Brown cow ! my love ! the milker of milk to thee !
> Ho ro ! my fair-skinned girl—a cow in the fold,
> And the birds have come !—glad sight I see !'

Eager to be of help, Alan put off in his boat and was soon among the fishermen, who in their new excitement were forgetful of all else than that the mackerel were come, and that every moment was precious. For the first time Alan found himself no unwelcome comrade. Was it, he wondered, because that there upon the sea whatever of shadow dwelt about him on the land was no longer visible?

All through that golden noon, he and the others worked hard. From isle to isle went the chorus of the splashing oars and splashing nets, of the splashing of the fish and the splashing of gannets and gulls, of the splashing of the tide leaping blithely against the sun-dazzle, and the innumerous rippling wash moving out of the west: all this blent with the loud joyous cries, the laughter and the hoarse shouts of the men of Barra and the adjacent islands. It was close upon dusk before the Rona boats put into the haven of Aonaig again: and by that time none was blither than Alan Carmichael, who in that day of happy toil had lost all the gloom and apprehension of the day before, and now made

o

haste to Caisteal-Rhona to add to his joy by a sight of Ynys in their home.

When, however, he got there, there was no Ynys to see. 'She had gone,' said Silis Macdonald, 'she had gone out in the smaller boat midway in the afternoon, and had sailed around to Aoidhu,'—the great scaur which ran out beyond the precipices at the southwest of Rona.

This Ynys often did : and of late more and more often.   Ever since she had come to the Hebrid Isles, her love of the sea had deepened, and had grown into a passion for its mystery and beauty.   Of late, too, something impelled to a more frequent isolation : a deep longing to be where no eye could see and no ear hearken. Those strange dreams which in a confused way had haunted her mind in her far Breton home, came oftener now and more clear.   Sometimes, when she had sat in the twilight at Kerival holding her mother's hand and listening to tales of that remote North to which her heart had ever yearned, she had suddenly lost all consciousness of the speaker, or of the things said, and had let her mind be taken captive by her uncontrolled imagination, till in spirit she was far away, and sojourned in strange places, hearing a language that she did not know, and yet which she understood, and dwelt in a past or a present which she had never seen and which yet was familiar.

Since Ynys had known she was with child, this visionariness had been intensified, this longing had become more and more a deep need. Even with Alan she felt at times the intrusion of an alien influence. If in her body was a mystery, a mystery also was in her brain and in her heart.

Alan knew this, and knowing, understood. It was for gladness to him that Ynys should do as she would: that in these long hours of solitude she drank deep of the elixir of peace: and that this way of happiness was open to her as to him. Never did these isolations come between them: indeed they were sometimes more at one then than when they were together, for all the deep happiness which sustained both upon the strong waters of their love.

So, when Alan heard from Silis that Ynys had sailed westward, he was in no way alarmed. But when the sun had set, and over the faint blue film

of the Isle of Tiree the moon had risen, and still
no sign of Ynys, he became restless and uneasy.
Silis begged him in vain to eat of the supper she
had prepared. Idly he moved to and fro along
the rocky ledge, or down by the pebbly shore, or
across the green airidh, eager for a glimpse of her
whom he loved so passing well.

At last, unable longer to endure a growing
anxiety, he put out in his boat, and sailed swiftly
before the slight easterly breeze which had prevailed since moonrise. So far as Aoidhu, all the
way from Aonaig, there was not a haven anywhere, nor even one of the sea-caverns which
honeycombed the isle beyond the headland. A
glance, therefore, showed him that Ynys had not
yet come back that way. It was possible, though
unlikely, that she had sailed right round Rona :
unlikely, because in the narrow straits to the
north, between Rona and the scattered islets
known as the Innse-mhara, strong currents prevailed, and particularly at the full of the tide,
when they swept north-eastward, dark and swift
as a mill-race.

Once the headland was passed, and the sheer

precipitous westward cliffs loomed black out of
the sea, he became more and more uneasy. As
yet there was no danger; but he saw that a swell
was moving out of the west, and whenever the
wind blew that way the sea-arcades were filled
with a lifting perilous wave, and escape from
them was difficult and often impossible. Out of
the score or more great corridors which opened
between Aoidhu and Ardgorm, it was difficult to
know into which to hazard entry in quest of
Ynys. Together they had examined all of them.
Some twisted but slightly, others wound sinu-
ously till the green serpentine alleys, flanked by
basalt walls hundreds of feet high, lost themselves
in an indistinguishable maze.

But that which was safest, and wherein a boat
could most easily make its way against wind or
tide, was the huge cavernous corridor known
locally as the Uamh-nan-roin, the Cave of the
Seals.

For this opening Alan steered his boat. Soon
he was within the wide corridor. Like the great
cave at Staffa, it was wrought as an aisle in some
natural cathedral; the rocks, too, were fluted

columnarly and rose in flawless symmetry as though
graven by the hand of man. At the far end of
this gigantic aisle, there diverges a long narrow
arcade, filled by day with the green shine of the
water, and by night when the moon is up with
a pale froth of light. It is one of the few
where there are open gateways for the sea and
the wandering light; and, by its spherical shape,
almost the only safe passage in a season of
heavy wind. Half-way along this arched arcade
a corridor leads to a round cup-like cavern,
midway in which stands a huge mass of black
basalt, in shape suggestive of a titanic altar.
Thus it must have impressed the imagination of
the islanders of old, for by them, even in a remote
day, it was called Teampull - nan - Mhara, the
Temple of the Sea. Owing to the narrowness
of the corridor, and to the smooth unbroken
walls which rise sheer from the green depths
into an invisible darkness, the Strait of the
Temple is not one wherein to linger long, save
in a time of calm.

Instinctively, however, Alan quietly headed his
boat along this narrow way. When, silently, he

emerged from the arcade, he could just discern the mass of basalt at the far end of the cavern. But there, seated in her boat, was Ynys: apparently idly adrift, for one oar floated in the water alongside, and the other suspended listlessly from the tholes.

His heart had a suffocating grip as he saw her whom he had come to seek. Why that absolute stillness, that strange listless indifference? For a dreadful moment, he feared that death had indeed come to her in that lonely place, where, as an ancient legend had it, a woman of old time had perished, and ever since had wrought death upon any who came thither solitary and unhappy.

But at the striking of the shaft of his oar against a ledge, Ynys gave a low cry, and looked at him with startled eyes. Half rising from where she crouched in the stern, she called to him in a voice that had in it something strangely unfamiliar.

'I will not hear,' she cried, 'I will not hear! Leave me! Leave me!'

Fearing that the desolation of the place had

wrought upon her mind, Alan swiftly moved towards her. The next moment his boat glided along hers. Stepping from the one to the other, he kneeled beside her.

' *Ynys-ghaolaiche*, Ynys my darling, what is it? what gives you dread? There is no harm here. All is well. Look! See, it is I, Alan, Alan, whom you love! Listen, dear, do you not know me, do you not know who I am? It is I, Alan, Alan who loves you!'

Even in that obscure light, he could clearly discern her pale face, and his heart smote him as he saw her eyes turn upon him with a glance wild and mournful. Had she indeed succumbed to the sea-madness which ever and again strikes into a terrible melancholy one here and there among those who dwell in the remote isles? But even as he looked, he noted another expression come into the beautiful eyes, and almost before he realised what had happened, Ynys's head was on his breast, and she sobbing with a sudden gladness and passion of relief.

The dusk deepened swiftly. In those ser-

pentine arcades darkness grows from hour to
hour, even on nights when the moon makes the
outer sea a blaze of silver fire. But sweet it was
to lie there in that solitary place, where no
sound penetrated save the low soughing sigh
of ocean, audible there only as the breath of a
sleeper; to lie there in each other's arms, and
to feel the beating of heart against heart,
knowing that whether in the hazard of life or
death all was well, since they two were there
and together.

For long, Ynys could say no word. And as
for Alan—too glad was he to have her again,
to know that she lived indeed, and that his fear
of the sea-madness was an idle fantasy; too glad
was he to urge her to speak, when her recovered
joy was still sweet in her heart. But at last she
whispered to him, how that she had sailed westward from Caisteal-Rhona, having been overcome
by the beauty of the day, and longing to be
among those mysterious green arcades where
thought rose out of the mind like a white bird,
and flew among shadows in strange places, bringing back with it upon its silent wings the rumour

of strange voices, and oftentimes singing a song of what ears hear not. Deeply upon the two had lain the thought of what was to be: the thought of the life she bore within her, that was the tangible love of her and of Alan, and yet was so strangely and remotely dissociate from either. Happy in happy thoughts, and strangely wrought by vague imaginings, she had sailed past precipice after precipice, and so at last into the Strait of the Temple. Just before the last light of day had begun to glide out of the pale green water, she had let her boat drift idly alongside the Teampull-Mhara. There, for a while, she had lain, drowsily content, dreaming her dream. Then, suddenly her heart had given a leap like a doe in the bracken, and the pulses in her veins swung like stars on a night of storm.

For there, in that nigh unreachable and forever unvisited solitude, was the figure of a man. He stood on the summit of the huge basalt altar, and appeared to have sprung from out of the rock; or, himself a shadowy presence, to have grown out of the obscure unrealities of the darkness. She had stared at him, fascinated, speechless.

When she had said this, Ynys stopped abruptly, for she felt the trembling of Alan's hand.

'Go on,' he said hoarsely, 'go on. Tell me all.'

To his amaze, she did not seem perturbed in the way he had dreaded when she began to tell what she had seen.

'But did you notice nothing about him, Ynys . . . about his face, his features?'

'Yes. His eyes filled me with strange joy.'

'With joy? O Ynys, Ynys, do you know whom—*what*—it was you saw? It was a vision, a nothingness, a mere phantom; and that phantom was . . . was . . . myself!'

'You, Alan! O no, Alan-aghray; dear, you do not know whom I saw—nor do I, though I know it was not you.'

'We will talk of this later, my fawn,' Alan muttered. 'Meanwhile, hold on to the ledge, for I wish to examine this mass of rock that they call the Altar.'

With a spring he was on the ledge. Then, swift and sure as a wild cat, he scaled the huge boulder.

Nothing ; no one. There was not a trace of any human being. Not a bird, not a bat; nothing. Moreover, even in that slowly blackening darkness he could see that there was no direct connection between the summit or side with the blank precipitous wall of basalt beyond. Overhead there was, so far as he could discern, a vault. No human being could have descended through that perilous gulf.

Was the island haunted, he wondered, as slowly he made his way back to the boat. Or had he been startled into some wild fantasy, and imagined a likeness where none had been? Perhaps, even, he had not really seen any one. He had read of similar strange delusions. The nerves can soon chase the mind into the dark zone wherein it loses itself.

Or was Ynys the vain dreamer? That, indeed, might well be, and she with child, and ever a visionary. Mayhap she had heard some fantastic tale from Morag MacNeill or from old Marsail Macrae: the islanders had *sgeul* after *sgeul* of a wild strangeness.

In silence he guided the boats back into the outer

arcade, where a faint sheen of moonlight glistered
on the water. Thence, in a few minutes, he
oared that wherein he and Ynys sat, with the
other fastened astern, into the open.

When the moonshine lay full on her face he
saw that she was thinking neither of him nor
of where she was. Her eyes were heavy with
dream.

What wind there was blew against their course,
so Alan rowed unceasingly. In silence they
passed once again the headland of Aoidhu : in
silence they drifted past a single light gleaming
in a croft near Aonaig, a red eye staring out into
the shadow of the sea from the room where the
woman Marsail lay dying ; and in silence their
keels grided on the patch of shingle in Caisteal-
Rhona haven.

But when, once more, Alan found himself with
Ynys in the safe quietudes of the haven, he
pressed her eagerly to give him some clear de-
scription of the figure she had seen.

Ynys, however, had become strangely reticent.
All he could elicit from her was that the man
whom she had seen bore no resemblance to him,

except in so far as he was fair. He was taller, slimmer, and seemed older.

He thought it wiser not to speak to her on what he himself had seen, or concerning his conviction that it was the same mysterious stranger who had appeared to both.

CHAPTER V

For days thereafter Alan haunted that rocky cavernous wilderness where he had seen the Herdsman.

It was in vain he had everywhere sought to find word of this mysterious dweller in those upland solitudes. At times he believed that there was indeed some one upon the island, of whom, for inexplicable reasons, none there would speak; but at last he came to the conviction that what he had seen was an apparition, projected by the fantasy of overwrought nerves. Even from the woman Morag MacNeill, to whom he had gone with a frank appeal that won its way to her heart, he learned no more than that an old legend, of which she did not care to speak, was in some way associated with his own coming to Rona.

Ynys, too, never once alluded to the mysterious incident of the green arcades which had so deeply impressed them both : never, that is, after the ensuing day which followed, when, simply and spontaneously, she told Alan that she believed that she had seen a vision. When he reminded her that she had been convinced of its reality, Ynys answered that for days past she had been dreaming a strange dream ; and that doubtless this had possessed her so that her nerves played her false in that remote and shadowy place. What this dream was she would not confide, nor did he press her.

But as the days went by, and as no word came to either of any unknown person upon the island, and as Alan, for all his patient wandering and furtive quest, both among the upland caves and in the Green Arcades, found absolutely no trace of him whom he sought, the belief that he had been duped by his imagination deepened almost to conviction.

As for Ynys, day after day soft veils of dream obscured the bare realities of life. But she, unlike Alan, became more and more convinced that

what she had seen was indeed no apparition. Whatever lingering doubt she had was
dissipated on the eve of the night when old
Marsail Macrae died. It was dusk when word
came to Caisteal-Rhona that Marsail felt the
cold wind on the soles of her feet. Ynys went
to her at once, and it was in the dark hour which
followed that she heard once more, and more
fully, the strange story which, like a poisonous
weed, had taken root in the minds of the
islanders. Already from Marsail she had heard
of the Prophet, though strangely enough she
had never breathed word of this to Alan, not
even when, after the startling episode of the
apparition in the Teampull-Mhara, she had, as
she believed, seen the Prophet himself. But
there in the darkness of the low turfed cottage,
with no light in the room save the dull red gloom
from the heart of the smoored peats, Marsail, in
the attenuated remote voice of those who have
already entered into the vale of the shadow, told
her this thing :—

'Yes, Ynys, wife of Alan MacAlasdair, I will

P

be telling you this thing before I change. You
are for knowing, sure, that long ago Uilleam,
brother of him who was father to your man, had
a son? Yes, you know that, you say, and also
that he was called Donnacha Bàn? No, mo-
run-geal, that is not a true thing that you have
heard, that Donnacha Bàn went under the wave
years ago. He was the seventh son, and was
born under the full moon: 'tis Himself will be
knowing whether that was for or against him.
Of these seven, none lived beyond childhood, except the two youngest, Kenneth and Donnacha.
Kenneth was always frail as a February flower,
but he lived to be a man. He and his brother
never spoke, for a feud was between them, not
only because that each was unlike the other, and
that the younger hated the older because thus
he was the penniless one—but most because
both loved the same woman. I will not be telling you the whole story now, for the breath in
my body will soon blow out in the draught that
is coming upon me; but this I will say to you,
darker and darker grew the gloom between these
brothers. When Kirsteen Macdonald gave her

love to Kenneth, Donnacha disappeared for a
time. Then one day he came back to Borosay,
and smiled quietly with his cold eyes when they
wondered at his coming again. Now, too, it was
noticed that he no longer had an ill-will upon
his brother, but spoke smoothly with him and
loved to be in his company. But to this day no
one knows for sure what happened. For there
came a gloaming when Donnacha Bàn came back
alone in his sailing-boat. He and Kenneth had
sailed forth, he said, to shoot seals in the sea-
arcades to the west of Rona, but in these
dark and lonely passages they had missed each
other. At last he had heard Kenneth's voice
calling for help, but when he had got to the
place it was too late, for his brother had been
seized with the cramps, and had sunk deep into
the fathomless water. There is no getting a
body again that sinks in these sea-galleries. The
crabs know that.

'Well, this and much more was what Donnacha
Bàn told to his people. None believed him;
but what could any do? There was no proof;
none had ever seen them enter the sea-caves

together. Not that Donnacha Bàn sought in any way to keep back those who would fain know more. Not so, he strove to help to find the body. Nevertheless, none believed; and Kirsteen nic Dhugall Mòr least of all. The blight of that sorrow went to her heart. She had death soon, poor thing; but before the cold greyness was upon her she told her father, and the minister that was there, that she knew Donnacha Bàn had murdered his brother. One might be saying these were the wild words of a woman; but, for sure, no one said that thing upon Borosay or Rona, or any of these isles. When all was done the minister told what he knew and what he thought to the Lord of the South Isles, and asked what was to be put upon Donnacha Bàn. "Exile for ever," said the Chief, "or if he stays here, the doom of silence. Let no man and woman speak to him or give him food or drink, or give him shelter, or let his shadow cross his or hers."

'When this thing was told to Donnacha Bàn Carmichael he laughed at first; but as day slid over the rocks where all days fall, he laughed no

more. Soon he saw that the Chief's word was
no empty word, and yet he would not go away
from his own place. He could not stay upon
Borosay, for his father cursed him; and no man
can stay upon the island where a father's curse
moves this way and that forever seeking him.
Then some say a madness came upon him, and
others that he took wildness to be his way,
and others that God put upon him the shadow
of loneliness, so that he might meet sorrow there
and repent. Howsoever that may be, Donnacha
Bàn came to Rona, and by the same token it
was the year of the great blight, when the
potatoes and the corn came to nought, and when
the fish in the sea swam away from the isles. In
the autumn of that year there was not a soul
left on Rona except Silis Macdonald and the old
man Ian, her father, who had guard of Caisteal-
Rhona for him who was absent. When, once
more, smoke rose from the crofts, the rumour
spread that Donnacha Bàn, the murderer, had
made his home among the caves of the upper
part of the isle. None knew how this rumour
rose, for he was seen of none. The last man

who saw him—and that was a year later—was
old Padruic M'Vurich, the shepherd.   Padruic
said that as he was driving his ewes across the
north slope of Ben Einaval in the gloaming he
came upon a silent figure seated upon a rock,
with his chin in his hands and his elbows on
his knees—with the great sad eyes of him staring
at the moon that was lifting itself out of the sea.
Padruic did not know who the man was.   The
shepherd had few wits, poor man; and he had
known, or remembered, little about the story of
Donnacha Bàn Carmichael, so when he spoke
to the man it was as to a stranger.   The man
looked at him and said:

'" You are Padruic M'Vurich, the shepherd."

'At that a trembling was upon old Padruic
who had the wonder that this stranger should
know who and what he was.

'" And who will you be, and forgive the saying?" asked he.

'"*Am Faidh*, the Prophet," the man said.

'"And what prophet will you be, and what is
your prophecy?" asked Padruic.

'" I am here because I wait for what is to be,

and that will be for the birth of a child that is to be a king."

'And with that, the man said no more, and the old shepherd went silently down through the hillside gloaming, and, heavy with the thoughts that troubled him, followed his ewes down into Aonaig. But after that neither he nor any other saw or heard aught of the shadowy stranger: so that all upon Rona felt sure that Padruic had beheld no more than a vision. There were some who thought that he had seen the ghost of the outlaw Donnacha Bàn: and mayhap one or two who wondered if the stranger that had said he was a prophet was not Donnacha Bàn himself, with a madness come upon him ; but at last these rumours went out to sea upon the wind, and men forgot. But—and it was months and months afterward, and three days before his own death— old Padruic M'Vurich was sitting in the sunset on the rocky ledge in front of his brother's croft, where then he was staying, when he heard a strange crying of seals. He thought little of that ; only, when he looked closer, he saw, in the hollow of the wave hard by that ledge, a drifting body.

'"*Am Faidh—Am Faidh!*" he cried, "the Prophet, the Prophet!"

'At that his brother and his brother's wife ran to see, but it was nothing that they saw. "It would be a seal," said Pol M'Vurich; but at that Padruic had shook his head, and said no, for sure, he had seen the face of the dead man, and it was of him whom he had met on the hillside, and that had said he was the Prophet who was waiting there for the birth of a king.

'And that is how there came about the echo of the thought, that Donnacha Bàn had at last, after his madness, gone under the green wave and was dead. For all that, in the months which followed, more than one man said he had caught a glimpse of a figure high up on the hill. The old wisdom says that when Christ comes again, or the Prophet who will herald Christ, it will be as a herdsman on a lonely isle. More than one of the old people on Rona and Borosay remembered that *sguel* out of the *seanachas* that the tale-tellers knew. There were some who said that Donnacha Bàn had never been drowned at all, and that he was this prophet, this Herdsman.

Others would not have that saying at all, but believed that the mysterious Herdsman was indeed Am Buchaille Bàn, the Fair-haired Shepherd, who had come again to redeem the people out of their sorrow. There were even those who said that the Herdsman who haunted Rona was no other than Kenneth Carmichael himself, who had not died, but had had the mind-dark there in the sea caves where he had been lost, and there had come to the knowledge of secret things, and so was at last *Am Faidh Chriosd.*'

A great weakness came upon the old woman when she had spoken thus far. Ynys feared that she would have breath for no further word, but after a thin gasping, and a listless fluttering of weak hands upon the coverlet, whereon her trembling fingers plucked aimlessly at the invisible blossoms of death, she opened her eyes once more and stared in a dim questioning at her who sat by her bedside.

'Tell me,' whispered Ynys, 'tell me, Marsail, what thought it is that is in your own mind?'

But already the old woman had begun to wander, though Ynys did not know this.

'For sure, for sure,' she muttered, '*Am Faidh* . . . *Am Faidh* . . . an' a child will be born . . . an' a king he will be, an' . . . that will be the voice of Domhuill, my husband, I am hearing . . . an' dark it is, an' the tide comin' in . . . an'——'

Then, sure, the tide came in, and if in that darkness old Marsail M'Vurich heard any voice at all, it was that of Domhuill who years agone had sunk into the wild seas off the head of Barra.

An hour later, with tears still in her eyes, Ynys walked slowly home through the cloudy night. All she had heard came back to her with a strange familiarity. Something of this, at least, she had known before. Some hints of this mysterious Herdsman had reached her ears. In some inexplicable way his real or imaginary presence there upon Rona seemed a pre-ordained thing for her. All that dreaming mysticism which had wrought so much of beauty and wonder into her girlhood in Brittany had expanded into a strange flower of the imagination—a flower whose subtle fragrance affected her inward life. Sometimes she had wondered if all the tragic vicissitudes which happened at Kerival, with the strange and dream-like life which she and Alan had led since, had so wrought upon her that the unreal became real, and the actual merely phantasmal; for now she felt more than ever assured that some hidden destiny had controlled all this disastrous mischance, had led her and Alan there to that lonely island.

She knew that the wild imaginings of the islanders had woven the legend of the Prophet, or at any rate of his message, out of the loom of the longing and the deep nostalgia whereon is woven that larger tapestry, the shadow-thridden life of the island Gael. Laughter and tears, ordinary hopes and pleasures, and even joy itself and bright gaiety, and the swift spontaneous imagination of susceptible natures—all this, of course, is to be found with the island Gael as with his fellows elsewhere. But, every here and there are some who have in their minds the inheritance from the dim past of their race, and are oppressed as no other people are oppressed, by the gloom of a strife between spiritual emotion and material facts. It is the brains of dreamers such as these which clear the mental life of the community; and it is in these brains are the mysterious looms which weave the tragic and sorrowful tapestries of Celtic thought. It were a madness to suppose that life in the isles consists of nothing but sadness and melancholy. It is not so, or need not be so, for the Gael is a creature of shadow and shine. But whatever the people is, the brain of the Gael hears a music that is sadder than any music there is, and has for its cloudy sky a gloom that shall not go, for the end is near, and upon the westernmost shores of these remote isles, the Voice—as has been truly said by one who has beautifully interpreted his own people—the Voice of Celtic Sorrow may be heard crying *Cha till, cha till, cha till mi tuille*— I will return, I will return, I will return no more.

Ynys knew all this well: and yet she too dreamed her Celtic dream—that, even yet, there might be redemption for the people. She did not share the wild hope which some of the older

islanders held, that Christ Himself shall come
again to redeem an oppressed race ; but might
not another Saviour arise, another redeeming
spirit come into the world? And if so, might
not that child of joy be born out of suffering
and sorrow and crime : and if so, might not that
child be born of her ?

With startled eyes, she crossed the thyme-set
ledge whereon stood Caisteal-Rhona. Was it,
after all, a message she had received from him
who appeared to her in that lonely cavern of the
sea : was he indeed *Am Faidh*, the mysterious
prophet of the isles ?

CHAPTER VI

WHAT are dreams but the dust of wayfaring thoughts? Or whence are they, and what air is upon their shadowy wings? Do they come out of the twilight of man's mind : are they ghosts of exiles from vanished palaces of the brain : or are they heralds with proclamations of hidden tidings for the soul that dreams?

It was a life of dream that Ynys and Alan lived : but Ynys the more, for, as week after week went by, the burden of her motherhood wrought her increasingly. Ever since the night of Marsail's death, Alan had noticed that Ynys no longer doubted but that in some way a special message had come to her, a special revelation. On the other hand, he had himself swung back to his former conviction : that the vision he had

seen upon the hillside was in truth that of a
living man. From fragments here and there, a
phrase, a revealing word, a hint gleaming through
obscure allusions, he came at last to believe that
some one bearing a close, and even extraordinary,
resemblance to himself lived upon Rona. Although
upon the island itself he could seldom per-
suade any one to speak of the Herdsman, the
islanders of Seila and Borosay became gradually
less reticent. He ascertained this, at least : that
their fear and aversion, when he first came, had
been occasioned by the startling likeness between
him and the mysterious being whom they called
Am Buchaille Bàn. On Borosay, he was told,
the fishermen believed that the *aonaran nan creag*,
the recluse of the rocks, as commonly they spoke
of him, was no other than Donnacha Bàn Carmichael, survived there through these many years,
and long since mad with his loneliness, and because of the burden of his crime. It was with
keen surprise that Alan learned how many of the
fishermen of Borosay and Berneray, and even of
Barra, had caught a glimpse of the outcast. It
was this relative familiarity, indeed, that was at

the root of the fear and aversion which had met
him upon his arrival. Almost from the moment
he had landed in Borosay, the rumour had spread
that he was indeed no other than Donnacha
Bàn, and that he had chosen this way, now both
his father and Alasdair Carmichael were dead,
to return to his own place. So like was Alan to
the outlaw who had long since disappeared from
touch with his fellow-men, that many were convinced the two could be no other than one
and the same. What puzzled him hardly less
was the fact that on the rare occasions when
Ynys had consented to speak of what she had
seen, the man she described bore no resemblance
to himself. From one thing and another, he
came at last to the belief that he had really
seen Donnacha Bàn, his uncle : but that the
vision of Ynys' mind was born of her imagination,
stimulated by all the tragedy and strange vicissitudes she had known, and wrought by the
fantastic tales of Marsail and Morag MacNeill.

By this time, too, the islanders had come to
see that Alan MacAlasdair was certainly not
Donnacha Bàn. Even the startling likeness no

longer betrayed them in this way. The ministers and the priests laughed at the whole story, and everywhere discouraged the idea that Donnacha Bàn could still be among the living. But for the unfortunate superstition that to meet the Herdsman, whether the lost soul of Donnacha Bàn, or indeed the strange phantom of the hills of which the old legends spoke, was to meet inevitable disaster: but for this, the islanders might have been persuaded to make such a search among the caves of Rona as would almost certainly have revealed the presence of any who dwelt therein.

But, as summer lapsed into autumn, and autumn itself through its golden silences waned into the shadow of the equinox, a quiet happiness came upon both Alan and Ynys. True, she was still wrought by her strange visionary life, though of this she said little or nothing : and, as for himself, he hoped that with the birth of the child this fantastic dream-life would go. Whoever the mysterious Herdsman was, if he indeed existed at all except in the imaginations of those who spoke of him either as the Buchaille Bàn or as the *aonaran nan chreag*, Alan believed that at last

Q

he had passed away. None saw him now : and
even Morag MacNeill, who had often on moonlight nights caught the sound of a voice chanting
among the upper solitudes, admitted that she
now heard nothing unusual.

St. Martin's Summer came at last, and with it
all that wonderful dreamlike beauty which bathes
the isles in a flood of golden light, and puts upon
sea and land a veil as of ineffable mystery.

One late afternoon, Ynys, returning to Caisteal-
Rhona after an unexplained absence of several
hours, found Alan sitting at a table. Spread before him were the sheets of one of the strange
old Gaelic tales which he had ardently begun to
translate. She took up the page which he had
just laid down. It was from the *Eachdaireachd
Challum mhic Cruimein,* and the last words that
Alan had translated were these :—

*' And when that king had come to the island, he
lived there in the shadow of men's eyes : for none
saw him by day or by night, and none knew
whence he came, or whither he fared : for his feet
were shod with silence, and his way with dusk.
But men knew that he was there, and all feared*

him. Months, even years, tramped one on the heels of the other, and perhaps the king gave no sign, but one day he would give a sign : and that sign was a laughing that was heard somewhere, be it upon the lonely hills or on the lonely wave, or in the heart of him who heard. And whenever the king laughed, he who heard would fare erelong from his fellows to join that king in the shadow. But sometimes the king laughed only because of vain hopes and wild imaginings, for upon these he lives as well as upon the strange savours of mortality.'

Ynys read the page over and over : and when Alan saw how she brooded upon it he regretted that he had left it for her to see.

He the more regretted this when he learned that on this very afternoon she had again been among the sea-caves. She would not say what she had seen or heard, if indeed she had heard or seen anything unusual. But that night she woke suddenly, and, taking Alan by the hand, made him promise to go with her on the morrow to the Teampull Mhara.

In vain he questioned her as to why she asked

this thing. All she would say was that she must go there once again, and with him, for she believed that a Spirit out of heaven had come to reveal to her a wonder. Distressed by what he knew to be a madness, and fearful that it might prove to be no passing fantasy, Alan would fain have persuaded her against this intention. Even as he spoke, however, he realised that it might be better to accede to her wishes, and above all to be there with her so that it might not be one only who heard or saw the expected revelation.

And it was a strange faring indeed, that which occurred on the morrow. At noon, when the tide was an hour turned in the ebb, they sailed westward from Caisteal-Rhona. It was in silence they made that strange journey together : for, while Alan steered, Ynys lay down in the hollow of the boat, with her head against his knees, and he saw that she slept, or at least lay still with her eyes closed.

When, at last, they passed the headland, and entered the first of the sea-arcades, she rose and sat beside him. Hauling down the now useless sail, he took an oar and, standing at the prow, urged the boat inward along the narrow corridor which led to the huge sea-cave of the Altar.

In the deep gloom, for even on that day of golden light and beauty the green air of the sea-cave was heavy with shadow, there was a deathly chill. What dull light there was came from the sheen of the green water which lay motionless along the black basaltic ledges. When, at last, the base of the Altar was reached, Alan secured the boat by a rope passed around a projecting spur : and then lay down in the stern beside Ynys.

' Tell me, dear, what is this thing that you expect to hear or see ? '

She looked at him strangely for a while, but though her lips moved she said nothing.

' Tell me, dear,' he urged again, ' who is it you expect to see or hear ? '

' *Am Buchaille Bàn*,' she answered, ' the Herdsman.'

For a moment he hesitated. Then, taking her hand in his, and raising it to his lips, he whispered in her ear—

'Dearest, all this is a vain dream. There is no Herdsman upon Rona. If ever there was a man there who lived solitary, if ever, indeed, there was an *aonaran nan chreag*, he is dead long since. What you have seen and heard has been a preying upon you of wild thoughts. Think no more of this vision. We have both suffered too much, and the knowledge of what is behind us has wrought upon us too hardly. It is a mistake to be here, on Rona, now. Ynys, darling, you and I are young, and we love : let us leave this melancholy isle, these melancholy isles, and go back into the green sunny world wherein we had such joy before : yes, let us even go back to Kerival, anywhere where we may live our life with joy and glad content—but not here, not in these melancholy haunted isles, where our dreams become more real than our life, and life itself, for us at least, the mere shadow of being. Ynys, will you come ? Will you go ?'

'All shall be as you will, Alan—afterwards. But first, I must wait here till our child is born, for I have heard that which is a message. And one part of that message concerns you and

me; and one concerns others. And that which
concerns you and me is that in this way, in
this child, to be born here in this place, lies
the redemption of the evil by which your father
was slain by my father. It is not enough that
you and I have forgotten the past; the past
remains. What we cannot do, or no man or
woman can do, the powers that are beyond the
grave can accomplish. Not our love, not even
ours, can redeem that crime. But if, born of
us, one will come, who will be dowered with
our love, and free from the blood-shadow which
lies upon us, then all will be well and the evil
shall be done with for evermore. But, also, has
not the prophet said that one shall be born upon
this island who will redeem his oppressed people?
and this prophet, Alan, I have seen and heard.
Never have I seen his face aright, for it has ever
been in the shadow; but I have heard his voice,
for he has spoken to me, and what he has said
is this: that in the fulness of time the child I
shall bear will be he of whom men have dreamed
in the isles for ages past. Sure, dear, you and
I must be believing that thing, since he who tells

it is no mere erring *Faidh,* but himself an immortal spirit.'

Alan looked at the speaker in amaze. There could be no question of her absolute sincerity; for the beautiful face was lit with a strange light, and in her eyes was a proud gleam of conscious sacrifice. That it was all a madness, a fantasy, he knew well. Long ago had Lois de Kerival spoken of the danger that lay for Ynys, she being the inheritor of a strange brooding spirit which belonged to her people. Now, in this remote place, the life of dream and the life of reality had become one; and Ynys was as a drifted ship among unknown seas and mists.

But on one point he believed he might convince her.

'Why do you speak of the Herdsman as spirit, Ynys? What proof have you of this? If you or I have seen any one at all, be sure it is a mortal man and no spirit; nay, I know who it must be if any one it is, for throughout the isles men say that Donnacha Bàn, the son of the brother of my father, was an outlaw here, and has lived long among the caves.'

'This man,' she said quietly, 'is not Donnacha Bàn, but the prophet of whom the people speak. He himself has told me this thing. Yesterday I was here, and he bade me come again. He spoke out of the shadow that is about the Altar, though I saw him not. I asked him if he were Donnacha Bàn, and he said no. I asked him if he were *Am Faidh*, and he said yes; I asked him if he were indeed an immortal spirit, and herald of that which was to be; and he said, even so!'

For a long while after this, no word was spoken betwixt the twain. The chill of that remote place began to affect Ynys, and she shivered slightly at times. But more she shivered because of the silence which prevailed, and because that he who had promised to be there gave no sign. Sure, she thought, it could not be all a dream; sure, the Herdsman would come again.

Then, at last, turning to Alan, she said, 'We must come on the morrow; for to-day, he is not here.'

'No, dear, never, never shall we come here again. This is for the last time. Henceforth, we shall dwell here in Rona no more.'

'You will do this thing for me, Alan, that I ask?'

'I will do what you ask, Ynys.'

'Then take this written word, and leave it upon the top of the great rock there that is called the Altar.'

With that she placed in his hand a slip of paper whereon she had already written certain words. What they were Alan could not discern in that shadowy light; but, taking the slip in his hand, he stepped on the black ledges at the base of the Altar, and slowly mounted the precipitous rock.

Ynys watched him till he became himself a shadow in that darkness. Her heart leaped when suddenly she heard a cry fall to her out of the gloom.

'Alan, Alan,' she cried—and a great fear was upon her when no answer came; but at last, with passionate relief, she heard him clambering slowly down the perilous slope of that obscure

place.   When he reached the ledge, he stood
still, regarding her.

'Why do you not come into the boat, Alan?'
she asked.

'Dear, I have that to tell you which will let
you see that I spoke truth.'

She looked at him with parted lips, her breath
coming and going like that of a caged bird.

'What is it, Alan?' she whispered.

'Ynys, when I reached the top of the Altar,
and in the dim light that was there, I saw the
dead body of a man lying upon the rock.   His
head was lain back so that the gleam from a
crevice in the cliff overhead fell upon it.   The
man has been dead many hours.   He is a man
whose hair has been greyed by years and sorrow,
but the man is he who is of my blood, he whom
I resemble so closely, he that the fishermen call
aonaran nan chreag, he that is the Herdsman.'

Ynys made no reply; still she looked at him
with large wondering eyes.

'Ynys darling, do you not understand what
it is that I say?   This man, that they call the
Buchaille Bàn—this man whom you believe to

be the Herdsman of the old legend—is no other than Donnacha Bàn, he who, years and years ago, slew his brother and has been an exile ever since on this lonely island.   How could he, then, a man as I am, though with upon him a worse blood-shadow than lies upon us, how could he tell you aught of what is to be?   What message could he give you that is himself a lost soul?

'Would you be for following a herdsman who could lead you to no fold?   This man is dead Ynys; and it is well that you brought me here to-day.   That is a good thing, and for sure God willed it.   Out of this all our new happiness may come.   For now we know what is this mysterious shadow that has darkened our lives ever since we came to Rona.   Now we have knowledge that it was no mere phantom I saw upon the hillside; and now also we know that he who told you these strange, wild things of which you speak, was no prophet with a message from the world of the spirit, but a man wrought to madness, a man who for all these years had lived his lonely secretive life upon the hills, or among these caves of the sea.   Come, then, dear, and let us ˌgo hence. Sure, at the last, it is well that we have found this way. Come, Ynys, we will go now and never come here again.'

He looked eagerly for her assenting eyes. With pain in his heart, however, he saw that the dream, the strange inexplicable fantasy, had not yet gone out of them. With a sigh, he entered the boat, and took her hand.

'Let us go,' she said, and that was all.

Slowly, Alan oared the boat across the shadowy gulf of the cave, along the narrow passage which led therefrom, and out into the pale green gloom of the arched arcade wherein the sight and sound of the sea made a music in his ears.

But the short November day was already passing to its end. All the sea westward was aflame with gold and crimson light, and in the great dome of the sky a wonderful radiance lifted above the paleness of the clouds whose pinnacled and bastioned heights towered in the south-west.

A faint wind blew eastwardly ; so, raising the sail, Alan made it fast and then sat down beside Ynys. But she, rising, moved along the boat to the mast, and leaned there with her face against the setting sun.

Idly they drifted onward. Deep silence prevailed betwixt them; deep silence was all about them, save for the endless inarticulate murmur of the sea, the splash of low waves against the rocks of Rona, and the sigh of the surf at the base of the basalt precipices.

And this was their homeward sailing on that day of revelation; Ynys, with her back against the mast, her face irradiated by the light of the setting sun; he, steering, with his face in shadow.

On a night of rain and amid the rumour of tempest, three weeks later, Ynys heard the laughter of the king, when the child, who was to be the bearer of so fair a destiny, lay by her side, white and chill as the foam thrown up for a brief while upon the rocks by the unheeding sea.

BOOK THIRD

THE BEAUTY OF THE WORLD

WHEN, once more, the exquisite mystery of Spring came upon the world, there was a not less wonderful rebirth in the heart of Ynys.

With the coming of that child upon whom such high hopes had been set—its birth, still and quiet as a snowdrop fallen before an icy wind upon the snow which nurtured it—all the fear of a mysterious Nemesis, because of her union with Alan, despite the shadow of tragic crime which made that union ominous of evil destiny; all the vague forebodings which had possessed her ever since she left Kerival; and, at the last, all the mystic elation with which her mind had become a winged and wandering spirit, passed from her.

The gloom of that northern winter was tonic to them both. As soon as her weakness was

past, and once more she was able to go about
with Alan, her old joyousness returned. In
her eyes it was almost as though the islanders
shared her recovered happiness. For one thing
they no more avoided her and Alan. With the
death of the man who had so long sustained
a mysterious existence upon Rona, their superstitious aversion went : they ceased to speak
of *Am Buchaille Bàn*; and, whether Donacha
Bàn had found on Rona one of the hidden ways
to heaven, or had only dallied upon one of the
byways to hell, it was commonly held that he
had paid his death-eric by his lonely and even
appalling life of unredeemed solitude. Now
that there was no longer any possibility of confusion between the outcast who had come to his
tragic end among the sea-caves of Rona, and his
kinsman who bore to him so extraordinary a
resemblance, a deep sense of the injustice that
had been done to Alan Carmichael prevailed
among the islanders. In many ways they showed
their regret; but most satisfactorily, so far as
Alan was concerned, by taking him as one of
themselves, as a man no longer under the shadow

of doom or in any way linked to a disastrous
fate.

True, there were still some of the islefolk on
Borosay and Barra who maintained that the man
who had been found in the sea-cave, whether
Donacha Bàn or some other, had nothing to do
with the mysterious herdsman, whose advent,
indeed, had long been anticipated by a section of
the older inhabitants. It was only seven years
since Murdo Macphail, better known as Murdo-
Bronnach-na-mhara, Brown Murdoch of the Sea,
from his habit of preaching to the islanders from
where he stood waist-deep in the water, had
prophesied that the Herdsman who was Shepherd
of Israel would indeed come again, and that
within seven years. And had he not added that
if the Fair Lonely One were not accepted of the
people, there would be deep sorrow for one and
all, and a bitter wrong upon all the isles of the
west ?

These murmurers now shook their heads, and
whispered often. Of a truth, they said, the Herdsman was come as foretold, and Alan Carmichael
was blind indeed not to see that Ynys, his wife,

had received a vision, and, because of her silence, been punished in the death of her first-born.

But with the white growth of winter the pleasant, familiar intercourse that everywhere prevailed wrought finally against the last threadbare fabric of superstition. Before the glow of the peats the sadness and gloom slowly dissipated. It was a new delight to both Alan and Ynys to find that the islanders could be so genial and almost gay, with a love of laughter and music and grotesque humour which even in the blithe little fishing haven of Ploumaliou they had never seen surpassed.

The cold months passed for them in a quiet content. That could not be happiness upon which was the shadow of so much pain: but there was something akin to it in the sweet serenity which came like calm after storm.

Possibly they might have been content to remain in Rona; to find in the island their interest and happiness. Ynys, indeed, often longed to leave the place where she had been so sadly disillusioned: and yet she did not urge that the home at Caisteal-Rhona should be broken up.

While they were still in this state of quiet suspense, news came that affected them strangely.

They had had no word from Kerival since they left. But one windy March day a boat from Borosay put into the haven with letters from Alan's agents in Edinburgh. Among them was one from the Abbé Caesar de la Bruyère, from Kerloek. From this, Alan learned strange news.

On the very day that he and Ynys had left Kerival, Annaik had disappeared. None knew where she had gone. At first it was thought that Judik Kerbastiou had something to do with her absence, but two days after she had gone he was again at Kerival. The house was a place of anarchy. No one knew whom to obey, what to do. With the Marquise Lois in her grave, with both Ynys and Annaik mysteriously absent, and apparently with no intention to return, and with Tristran the Silent more morosely taciturn than his wont and more than ever an invalid, with all this it was difficult for those in authority to exact the habitual duties. But in addition to this there were the imperious claims of Judik

Kerbastiou, emphasised by his refusal to be addressed by any other name than the Sieur Jud de Kerival.

When, suddenly, and while quietly dictating a letter, the Marquis Tristran died, it seemed at last as though Judik's triumph had come. For a brief while he was even addressed as Monsieur le Marquis. But on the noon following that day he had a rude awakening. A notary from Ploumaliou arrived with the family lawyers, and produced a written and signed confession on the part of the woman whom he had called mother that he was not her child at all, that her own child was dead, and that Kerbastiou was really a forest foundling. As if this were not enough, the notary also proved, even to the conviction of Judik, that the written marriage-testimony from the parish books was an impudent forgery.

So the man who had made so abrupt and dramatic an appearance on the threshold of Kerival had, in the very moment of his triumph, to retreat once more to his obscurity as a homeless woodlander.

The sole heirs now were Annaik and Ynys,

but of neither was anything known. The difficulty was partially solved by the abrupt appearance of Annaik on the day of the second conclave.

For a time thereafter all went well at Kerival. Then rumour began to spread mysterious whispers about the lady Annaik. She would see none of her neighbours, whether from far or near, and even the Sieur de Morvan and his kith or kin were denied. Then, too, she disappeared for days at a time. Some thought she went to Ploumaliou or Kerloek, some that she had gone as far away as Rennes or St. Brieuc, and a few even imagined the remote Paris to be her goal. None dreamed that she had gone no further than the forest of Kerival.

But, as the autumn waned, rumours became more explicit. Strange things were said of Annaik de Kerival. At last the anxious Curé of Ploumaliou took it upon himself to assure all who spoke to him about the lady of Kerival that he had good reason to believe she was privately married. This at least drew some of the poison out of the gossip which had arisen.

Then a day came when the lady Annaik dismissed the servants at Kerival, and left none in the house save an old gardener and his wife. She was going away for a time, she said. She went, and from that day was not seen again.

Then came, in the Abbé Caesar de la Bruyère's letter, the strangest part of the mystery.

Annaik, ever since the departure of Alan and Ynys, had been living the forest life. All her passionate sylvan and barbaric instincts had been suddenly aroused. For the green woods and the forest ways she suffered an intolerable nostalgia. But over and above this, was another reason. It seemed, said the Abbé Caesar, that she must have returned the rude love of Judik Kerbastiou. However this might be, she lived with him for days at a time, and he himself had a copy of their marriage-certificate made out at a registrar's in a remote little hill-town in the Montagnes Noires.

This union with the morose and strange Judik Kerbastiou had not been known to any of the peasants until her trouble came to her. When the day was near she did not return to Kerival, but kept to the gypsy-tent which she shared with

Judik. After the birth of the child, every one knew, and every one marvelled. It was a madness: that was what all said, from Kerloek to Ploumaliou.

But neither the union nor the child brought happiness to these twain, so much at one in their woodland life, so hopelessly alien in all else. One day a man named Iouenn Kerbac'h, passing by the tent where Judik and Annaik had taken shelter from a violent thunderstorm, overheard a savage upbraiding on the part of Kerbastiou. Annaik was his wife, it was true—so he cried— but a wife who had in nothing short of madness renounced everything, and now would claim nothing of her own nor allow him to claim aught: a wife whom he loved with another madness, and yet hated because she was so hopelessly remote from himself: a wife who had borne a child, but a child that had nothing of the gypsy eyes and swarthy darkness of Judik Kerbastiou, but was fair, and with skin as white and eyes as blue as those of Alan de Kerival.

It was this, and the terrible words that were said, which made Iouenn Kerbac'h hurry onward, dreading to listen further. Yet nothing that he overheard gave him so strange a fear as the laugh with which Annaik de Kerival greeted a savage screaming threat of death, hurled at her because of her silence after the taunting accusation he had made . . . had made, and denied her to refute.

None heard or saw Annaik Kerbastiou after that day, till the night of the evening when Judik came into Haut-Kerloek, and went straight to Jehan Rusgol the Maire.

When asked what he had come for, he had replied simply, 'The woman Annaik is dead.' It was commonly thought that he had killed her, but there was no evidence of this, and the end of the inevitable legal procedure was the acquittal of the woodlander. From that day the man was rarely seen of his fellows, and even then, for the most part, only by charcoal-burners and others who had forest-business. A few peasants knew where his hut was, and now and again called to speak with him, or to drink a cup of cider; but oftener than not he was absent, and always with the child. The boy had survived his mother's death, and in some strange way had suddenly become so dear to Judik Kerbastiou that the two were inseparable.

This, then, was the tidings which startled Alan and Ynys out of their remote quiescence.

The unexpected news, coupled with the urgent request that both should return to Kerival, if only for a brief while, so as to prevent the property falling into absolute ruin, came as a whip upon Alan's mind. To all he said, Ynys agreed, and was even glad to leave Rona and return to Brittany.

So it was that, with the first days of April, they bade farewell to Ian and his sister, whom they left at Caisteal-Rhona, which was henceforth to be their home, and to all upon the island, and set forth in a fishing smack for Borosay.

It was not till the last of the precipices of Rona was lost to view behind the south headland of Borosay that Ynys clearly realised the deep gladness with which she left the lonely Isle of the Caves. That it would have been impossible for her to live there long she was now well assured; and for Alan, too, the life was not

suitable.   For the north, and for the islands, they
would ever have a deep feeling almost sacred in
its intensity; but all that had happened made
living there a thing difficult and painful for
them; and, moreover, each, though Ynys most,
missed that green woodland beauty, the ceaseless forest charm, which made the very memory
of Kerival so fragrant.

They went away, then, not as travellers who
fare far with no thought of return, but rather
as pilgrims returning homeward from a shrine
sacred to them by profound and intimate associa-
tions.

That was indeed for them a strange home-
going.   From the first there was something
dreamlike, unreal, about that southward flight;
in the long sail across Hebrid seas, calm as glass
until the south headlands of Mull were passed,
and then storm-swept; in the rapid journey
across Scotland and through England; and in
the re-crossing of that narrow sea which had
once seemed to them a gulf of ultimate division.

But when once more they saw the grotesque
bulbous spire of Ploumaliou rising above the

sand-dunes, by which, from St. Malo, they approached the dear familiar country, all this uncertainty went from them. With light hearts they realised it was indeed true, that they were free at last of a life for which they were now unfitted, and that the lost threads in the maze had been found.

By their own wish the home-coming was so private that none knew of it save the doctor, the curé, the lawyer who accompanied them from Ploumaliou, and the old gardener and his wife. As they neared the château from the north, Alan and Ynys alighted from the dishevelled carriage, which was the sole vehicle of which Ploumaliou could boast. M. Auriol could drive on alone : for themselves, they chose to reach their home by the dunes and scattered pines, and thence by the yew-close behind the manor-house.

The day was windless, and of a serene beauty. Ever since noon the few clouds, suspensive in the azure flood like islets of snow, had waned, till they were faint and light as blown swans-down, then filmy as vapour lifted against the

sun, and at last were no more visible, there had
been the same unfathomable depths of azure,
through which the tides of light imperceptibly
ebbed from the zenith. The sea, too, was of a
vivid though motionless blue, save where luminous with a white sheen, or wrought with violet
shadows and straits of amethyst. Upon the
land lay a golden peace. A richer glow involved the dunes, where the pine-shadows cast
long motionless blue shapes. As, hand in hand,
Ynys and Alan moved athwart the pine-glade,
whence they could pass at once either westward
into the cypress-alley or eastward through the
yew-close, they stopped instinctively. Beyond
them rose the chimneys and gables of the
House of Kerival, strangely still and remote for
all their familiar look. What a brief while ago
it seemed since he and she had walked under
these pines, wrought by the first ecstasy of their
virginal love! Then those who now lay quiet
in the darkness of the earth were alive: Lois de
Kerival, with her repressed passionate heart still
at last; the Marquis Tristran, with the young
grass growing soft and green over his bitter-

ness; Alasdair Carmichael, with the echo of the island waves stilled under the quiet bells of the little church which guarded the graveyard of St. Blaise; and Annaik, poor lost waif of beautiful womanhood, submerged for ever in the green woods she loved so well, and sleeping so sound a sleep at last in an unmarked hollow beneath an ancient tree in some obscure glade or alley.

A shadow was in Alan's eyes, a deeper shadow than that caused by thought of the dead, who lay heedless and listless at once so near and yet such depths away—a deeper shadow than that cast by memory of the crime which overlay the past.

As his eyes wandered to the cypress-alley, his heart knew again a pain almost beyond endurance: a pain that only the peace of Rona had translated into a strong acquiescence in the irrevocable past, a pain become less haunting under the stress of all which had happened in connection with the Herdsman, till it knew a bitter resurrection when Alan came to read of the tragic fate of the woman who had loved him.

Through some wayward impulse, Ynys abruptly

asked him to go with her through the cypress-
alley, so that they should approach the château
from the forest.

Silently, and with downcast eyes, he walked by
her side, his hand still in hers. But his thoughts
were with the dead woman, on the bitter hazard
of love, and on what lay, for ever secret, between
Annaik and himself. And as he communed with
himself, in an austere pain of remembrance, he
came to see more and more clearly that in some
strange way the Herdsman-episode, with all
involved therein, was no arbitrary chance in the
maze of life, but a definite working out of destiny. None could ever know what Annaik had
foretold, had known, on that terrible night when
the silence of the moonlit peace was continuously
rent by the savage screams of the peacocks; nor
could any other than himself discern, against the
dark tapestries of what veiled his inner life, the
weaving of an inextricable web.

It was difficult for him to believe that she was·
dead—Annaik, who had always been so radiantly,
superbly alive. Now there was dust upon that
wonderful bronze hair, darkness upon those lam-

bent eyes, no swift pulse beating in the red tide in the veins, a frost against the heart. What a burden it had carried, poor heart! O Annaik, Annaik, he muttered below his breath, what a hard wayfaring because of a passion crucified upon the bitter tree of despair; what a fierce, silent, unwavering tyranny over the rebellious voices crying unceasingly from every nerve, or swept this way and that on every stormy tide of blood!

That Annaik who loved the forest so passing well, and in whom the green fire of life flamed consumingly, should no longer be alive to rejoice in the glory of Spring, now once again everywhere involving the brown earth and the purple branches, was almost unrealisable. To walk in that cypress-alley once more, to cross that open glade with its single hawthorn, to move in the dark-green shadow of that yew-close, to do this and remember all that Annaik had suffered, and that now she lay quiet and beyond all pain or joy to touch her, was to Alan a thought almost too poignant to be borne.

It was with an effort he answered Ynys when

S

she spoke, and it was in silence that they
entered the house which was now their home,
and where—years ago, as it seemed—they had
been young and happy.

But that night he sat alone for a time in the
little room in the tower which rose from the east
wing of Kerival—the room he had fitted up as an
observatory, similar on a smaller scale to that in
the Tour de l'Ile, where he had so deeply studied
the mystery of the starry world. Here he had
dreamed many dreams, and here he dreamed yet
another.

For out of his thoughts about Annaik and
Ynys arose a fuller, a deeper conception of
womanhood. How well he remembered a legend
that Ynys had told him on Rona: a legend of
a fair spirit which goes to and fro upon the
world, the Weaver of Tears. He loves the pathways of sorrow. His voice is low and sweet, with
a sound like the bubbling of waters in that fount
whence the rainbows rise. His eyes are in quiet
places, and in the dumb pain of animals as in
the agony of the human brain: but most he is
found, oftenest are the dewy traces of his feet,
in the heart of woman.

Tears, tears: they are not the saltest tears which are on the lids of those who weep. Fierce tears there are, hot founts of pain in the mind of many a man, that are never shed, but slowly crystallise in furrows on brow and face, and in deep weariness in the eyes : fierce tears, unquench-able, in the heart of many a woman, whose brave eyes look fearlessly at life, whose dauntless courage goes forth daily to die but never to be vanquished.

In truth the Weaver of Tears abides in the heart of woman. O Mother of Pity, of Love, of deep Compassion : with thee it is to yearn for ever for the ideal human, to bring the spiritual love into fusion with human desire, endlessly to strive, endlessly to fail, always to hope in spite of disillusion, to love unswervingly against all baffling and misunderstanding, and even forget-fulness ! O Woman, whose eyes are always stretched out to her erring children, whose heart is big enough to cover all the little chil-dren in the world, and suffer with their sufferings, and joy with their joys : Woman, whose other divine names are Strength and Patience, who is no girl, no virgin, because she has drunk too deeply of the fount of Life to be very young or very joyful. Upon her lips is the shadowy kiss of death: in her eyes is the shadow of birth. She is the veiled interpreter of the two mysteries. Yet what joyousness like hers, when she wills: because of her unwavering hope, her inexhaustible fount of love?

So it was that just as Alan had long recognised as a deep truth, how the spiritual nature of man has been revealed to humanity in many divine incarnations, so he had come to believe that the spiritual nature of woman has been revealed in the many Marys, sisters of the Beloved, who have had the keys of the soul and the heart in their unconscious keeping. In this exquisite truth, he knew a fresh and vivid hope. Was it all a dream that Ynys had dreamed, far away among the sea-arcades of Rona? Had the Herdsman, the Shepherd of Souls, indeed revealed to her that a child was to be born who would be one of the Redeemers of the world? A Woman-Saviour, who would come near to all of us, because in her heart would be the blind tears of the child, and the bitter tears of the man, and the patient tears of the woman : who would be the Compassionate One, with no end or aim but compassion—with no doctrine to teach, no way to show, but only deep, wonderful, beautiful, inalienable, unquench-able compassion ?

For in truth there is the divine eternal femi-nine counterpart to the divine eternal male, and both are needed to explain the mystery of the dual spirit within us—the mystery of the two in one, so infinitely stranger and more wonderful than that triune life which the blind teachers of the blind have made a rock of stum-bling and offence out of a truth clear and obvious as noon.

We speak of Mother Nature, but we do not discern the living truth behind our words. How few of us have the vision of this great brooding Mother, whose garment is the earth and sea, whose head is pillowed among the stars : she who, with death and sleep as her familiar shapes, soothes and rests all the weariness of the world, from the waning leaf to the beating pulse, from the brief span of a human heart to the furrowing of granite brows by the uninterrupted sun, the hounds of rain and wind, and the untrammelled airs of heaven.

Not cruel, relentless, impotently anarchic, chaotically potent, this Mater Genetrix. We see her thus, who are flying threads in the loom she weaves. But she is patient, abiding, certain, inviolate, and silent ever. It is only when we come to this vision of her whom we call Isis, or Hera, or Orchil, or one of a hundred other names, our unknown Earth-Mother, that men and women will know each other aright, and go hand in hand along the road of life without striving to crush, to subdue, to usurp, to retaliate, to separate.

Ah, fair vision of humanity to come : man and woman side by side, sweet, serene, true, simple, natural, fulfilling earth's and heaven's behests, unashamed, unsophisticated, unaffected, each to each and for each, children of one mother, inheritors of a like destiny, and, at the last, artificers of an equal fate.

Pondering thus, Alan rose, and looked out into the night. In that great stillness, wherein the moonlight lay like the visible fragrance of the earth, he gazed long and intently. How shadowy, now, were those lives that had so lately palpitated in this very place: how strange their silence, their incommunicable knowledge, their fathomless peace !

Was it all lost . . . the long endurance of pain, the pangs of sorrow ? If so, what was the lesson of life ? Surely to live with sweet serenity and gladness, content against the inevitable hour. There is solace of a kind in the idea of a common end, of that terrible processional march of life wherein the myriad is momentary, and the immeasurable is but a passing shadow. But, alas, it is only solace of a kind : for what heart that has beat to the pulse of love can relinquish the sweet dream of life, and what coronal can philosophy put upon the brows of youth in place of eternity ?

No, no : of this he felt sure. In the Beauty of the World lies the ultimate redemption of our mortality. When we shall become at one with nature in a sense profounder even than the poetic imaginings of most of us, we shall understand what now we fail to discern. The arrogance of those who would have the stars as candles for our night, and the universe as a pleasaunce for our thought, will be as impossible as their blind fatuity who say we are of dust, briefly vitalised, that shall be dust again, with no fragrance saved from the rude bankruptcy of life, no beauty raised up against the sun to bloom anew.

It is no idle dream, this : no idle dream that we are a perishing clan among the sons of God, because of this slow waning of our joy, of our passionate delight, in the Beauty of the World. We have been unable to look out upon the shining of our star, for the vision overcomes us; and we have used veils which we call 'scenery,' 'picturesqueness,' and the like—poor barren words that are so voiceless and remote before the rustle of leaves and the lap of water, before the ancient music of the wind, and all the sovran eloquence of the tides of light. But a day may come—nay, shall surely come—when indeed the poor and the humble shall inherit the earth: they who have not made a league with temporal evils and out of whose heart shall arise the deep longing, that shall become universal, of the renewal of youth.

Often, in the days which followed their return to Kerival, Alan and Ynys talked of these hopes and fears. And, gradually, out of the beauty of the Spring, out of the intensity of the green fire of life which everywhere flamed in the brown earth, on the hills, in the waters, in the heart and brain of man, in the whole living, breathing world, was born of them a new joy. They were as the prince and princess of the fairy tales, for whom everything was wonderful. Hand in hand they entered into the kingdom of youth. It was theirs, thenceforth : and all the joy of the world.

To live, and love, and be full of a deep joy, a glad content, a supporting hope! What destiny among the stars fairer than this?

They would be harbingers of joy. That was what they said, one to another. They would be so glad with sweet life, that others would rejoice: out of their strength they would strengthen, out of their joy they would gladden, out of their peace they would comfort, out of their knowledge they would be compassionate.

Nor was their dream an unfulfilled vision. As the weeks slipped into months, and the months lapsed into years, Alan and Ynys realised all it is possible for man and woman to know of happiness. Happiness, duties, claims, held them to Kerival: but there they lived in fair comradeship with their fellows, with the green forest, with all that nature had to give them for their delight through wind and wave, through shadow and shine, through changing seasons and the exquisite hazard of every passing hour.

To them both, too, came the added joy which they feared had been forfeited at Rona. When Ynys felt the child's hand on her breast, she was as one transformed by a light out of heaven. Alan, looking at mother and child, understood, with all his passion for the intimate wonder and mystery of nature, the deeper truth in the words of one of the greatest of men . . . ' The Souls of the Living are the Beauty of the World.'

That, sometimes, a shadow fell was inevitable. None ever so dusked the sunway of Alan's mind as when, remote in the forest of Kerival, he came upon the unkempt figure of Judik Kerbastiou, often carrying upon his shoulder a little child, whose happy laughter was sweet to hear, in whose tawny hair was a light such as had gleamed in Annaik's, and whose eyes were blue as the north sea's and as Alan's were.

Often, too, alone in his observatory, where he was wont to spend much of his time, Alan knew that strange nostalgia of the mind for impossible things. Then, wrought for a while from his vision of green life, and flamed by another green fire than that born of the earth, he dreamed his dream. With him, the peopled solitude of night was a concourse of confirming voices. He did not dread the silence of the stars, the cold remoteness of the stellar fire.

In that other watch-tower in Paris, where he had spent the best hours of his youth, he had loved that nightly watch of the constellations. Now, as then, in the pulse of the planets he found assurances which faith had not given him. In the vast majestic order of that nocturnal march, that diurnal retreat, he had learned the law of the whirling leaf and the falling star, of the slow æon-delayed comet and of the slower wane of solar fires. Looking with visionary eyes into that

congregation of stars, he realised, not the little-
ness of the human dream but its divine impulsion.
It was only when, after long vigils into the
quietudes of night, he turned his gaze from the
palaces of the unknown, and thought of the
baffled fretful swarming in the cities of men,
that his soul rose in revolt against the sub-
lime ineptitude of man's spiritual leaguer against
destiny.

Destiny—' An Dan '—it was a word familiar to
him since childhood, when first he had heard it
on the lips of old Ian Macdonald.   And once, on
the eve of the Feast of Paschal, when Alan had
asked Daniel Darc what was the word which the
stars spelled from zenith to nadir, the astronomer
had turned and answered simply, ' C'est le Destin.'

But Alan was of the few to whom this talis-
manic word opens lofty perspectives, even while
it obscures those paltry vistas which we deem
unending and dignify with vain hopes and void
immortalities.

Printed by T. and A. CONSTABLE, Printers to Her Majesty
at the Edinburgh University Press

OPINIONS OF THE PRESS

ON THE WRITINGS OF

FIONA MACLEOD

'Not beauty alone, but that element of strangeness in beauty which Mr. Pater rightly discerned as the inmost spirit of romantic art—it is this which gives to Miss Macleod's work its peculiar æsthetic charm. But apart from and beyond all those qualities which one calls artistic, there is a poignant human cry, as of a voice with tears in it, speaking from out a gloaming which never lightens to day, which will compel and hold the hearing of many who to the claims of art as such are wholly or largely unresponsive. If I were to ask myself what were the external objects of contemplation which have most strongly influenced Miss Macleod, I should say, first, wild nature, felt not as a mere show of beauty or of wonder, but as a presence and a power ; second, the tragic pathos always cunningly interwoven with the fabric of human passion and human fate ; and, third—though this, indeed, is hardly distinct from the second—the strange, barbaric element, which sometimes breaks up even the thick crust of an elaborated civilisation, though it can naturally be observed most steadily and studied most closely among the unsophisticated, simple, elemental human beings who live not merely *with* Nature, but, so to speak, *in* her, and feel the stirrings of a conscious kinship. . . . The Gaelic nature is in some ways markedly un-Hellenic, and yet I think we have to go back to Greek tragedy for a rendering of the irresistible dominance of fate equal in imaginative impressiveness to some of her celebrations of the Western Gael's persistently fatalistic outlook upon human life.'—*James Ashcroft Noble in 'The New Age.'*

OPINIONS OF THE PRESS

'Recently a new element has been introduced into Scottish fiction, which bids fair to assume proportions of considerable importance. A novelist of the romantic order has arisen, who gives promise of making a permanent mark not only in Highland but in English literature. Miss Fiona Macleod has given to the world four works which, one may well believe, have laid the foundation of a great reputation.'—*Mr. William C. Mackenzie in ' The Highland News.'*

'The most remarkable figure in the Scottish Celtic Renascence, Miss Fiona Macleod, has now set three books before the public, and it is time to appraise her seriously.'—*From an article on Fiona Macleod and the Celtic Renascence, in ' The Irish Independent.'*

'It is impossible to read her and not to feel that some magic in her touch has made the sun seem brighter, the grass greener, the world more wonderful.'—*Mr. George Cotterell in an article in ' The Academy.'*

'Miss Fiona Macleod's second book, *The Mountain Lovers*, fully justifies the opinions already formed of her exquisite handicraft. . . . Her vocabulary, in particular, is astonishing in its range, its richness, and its magic: she seems to employ every beautiful word in the English language with instinctive grace and sense of fitness.'—*Mr. Grant Allen in an article entitled ' The Fine Flower of Celticism.'*

'The fascination of "atmosphere" in all Miss Macleod's work is extraordinary.'—*Mr. H. D. Traill in the ' Graphic.'*

'For sheer originality, other qualities apart, her tales are as remarkable, perhaps, as anything we have had of the kind since Mr. Kipling appeared. . . . Their local colour, their idiom, their whole method, combine to produce an effect which may be unaccustomed, but is therefore the more irresistible. They provide as original an entertainment as we are likely to find in this lingering century, and they suggest a new romance among the potential things of the century to come.'—*The Academy.*

'Of the products of what has been called the Celtic Renascence, *The Sin-Eater* and its companion stories seem to us the most remarkable. They are of imagination and a certain terrible beauty all compact.'—*From an article in ' The Daily Chronicle' on ' The Gaelic Glamour.'*

THE WASHER OF THE FORD:

AND OTHER LEGENDARY MORALITIES AND TALES

' In power of treatment, in the fierce imaginative realism of some of them, and the profound depth of sadness or bitterness in others, her earlier writings bore fresh witness to the genius which by that time most of her critics recognised in Miss Macleod's work. But some of us still looked for a fuller revelation . . . and this fuller revelation we have in the present volume.'—*The Academy.*

' Miss Macleod's new book persuades one more than ever that she is the possessor of that rare and precious thing, genius. . . . This new work has energy, passion, beauty, and sweetness.'—*The National Observer.*

' Few are the thankful days when one finds an arresting new book that has all the force and circumstance and vitality of insight, of art ; that is, an inspired voice, not an intellectual accident ; a medium for a little gracious lore from Being's secret places ; a vehicle for a spirit that is infused and quickened with some sense of subsided waters in which eternal verities are at anchor. The sense of all this, and of certain other magical qualities, we have come to expect in the work of that singularly gifted young writer, Miss Fiona Macleod, whose progress will give the material for perhaps the most charming chapter in the story of the closing century's literature.'—*The Sun.*

' " There is no mystery in them, or anywhere, except the eternal mystery of beauty "—and Miss Macleod certainly possesses the master-key to the heart of that mystery. We are moved by the same imaginative vision, the same passionate sympathy with the elemental forces of nature, and the imperishable primeval human passions.'—*The Daily Chronicle.*

' Literary watchers for signs on the horizon may well acclaim these stories, and call them, if they will, the Celtic Renascence— though here is indeed a renascence, as all romance is a renascence : —a less ambitious and perhaps truer philosophy will be content to say that these are eternal elements of poetry, and the name of the present avatar is not a concatenation of abstract terms, but simply Miss Fiona Macleod.'—*The Manchester Guardian.*